Microchip + Tribulation

Audrey Andujar Wright

Cover illustration entitled: "The Book of Knowledge," by Anastashya Andujar.

Personal Memoirs/Religion/Poetry
ISBN: 10-1517121337
ISBN-13: 978-1517121334

DEDICATION

This book is dedicated as a legacy for Jean Brown
(Mother Jean).

CONTENTS

1 TRIBULATION TIPS

You may notice men/women throwing themselves at you. Be careful whom you allow to gain your trust, remember, all of their actions and reactions may not necessarily be under their control at all times. Use your gift of discernment and remember The Word says, Trust only the Lord. Google "Snowden Honey Trap." You'll want to avoid being discredited and appearing violent or volatile.

Don't ever put it past anyone that the end result, no matter how innocent the beginning aim, might be for you to utter a self-damning confession about anything and that it may be used against you if not in a court of law, possibly in the court of public opinion. Think poor Jimmy Swaggart, but be thankful for his resulting growth and how the Lord has blessed us through him over the years.

Forgo online dating if you're single, and give up sex. Pray a lot.

Don't get massages or anything else that leaves you naked and vulnerable.

Beware of "neighbors," especially those who come over to talk and ask questions for hours, but love them, in the Christian sense and pray for them. Deliver the "Good News," if they are not yet saved.

Choose your friends carefully, try to stick with those you knew growing up. But choose your words carefully and trust no one— not kids, not parents, not dogs, not even Ushers.

Should strangers approach you in public places, be polite and curt, don't engage in meaningless conversations unless moved to give a word by the Spirit of God. At all costs, try not to offend, and if you have nothing good to say, try to separate yourself from them expediently and politely. If they start to touch you or to invade your personal space, bless them with your whole heart and politely say and mean "God bless you, have a nice day." Remember, you don't know what they are going through.

Try not to entertain, but if you decide to, submit yourself and everyone where you are to the Lord in prayer and beg for His will to be done in and through all of you.

Don't entertain "telemarketers," but *always* be polite with everyone on the phone and in person.

If you notice strangers taking pictures of you, put your chin up, suck it in, and smile. Every photo you take is a declaration (literally), choose your background and expressions wisely.

If you suspect you are under surveillance, don't get upset. Many times people with limited knowledge of the whole are sent to do very limited tasks and only you feel the compounded effects. If in fact they are being "sent" to destabilize you, recognize that they don't know it all; they are doing a job, and they have to eat too. Pray for them. Bless them with your whole heart, forgive
them, and move on. Recognize that they may be carrying a great weight too, and that some are being manipulated themselves. Do not lose patience or faith; God can turn everything to good for
you and for them.

The tags in the cars around you every now and then will make you think you've lost your mind as they will be abbreviations for things only you may recognize. These could be very personal, and the aim might be to make you lose your patience (your cool) and force you to do something stupid, like speed or ram into something.

Sometimes, you may be Tailgated or feel endangered as if someone is trying to crash into your vehicle when you're turning unto your street or places you visit regularly, sometimes they'll try
to side swipe you. Keep praying and forgiving, and know the more driving incidents you permit yourself to have, the better a case could be made in the future of your own fault should anything actually happen to you in a car—or you may lose your license, mobility and independence: pray and forgive.

If someone starts to cross the street in front of your car in a parking lot, slow down and let them pass.
Don't honk your horn unless you have to.

Approach intersections with lights carefully, they tend to change from green to red quickly sometimes.

Discern when to use rush hour to your advantage.

Don't use your phone while you're driving, not even at stop lights. Pull over if you need to make a call. "Smart Phones" are only smart for those controlling them. Get an old flip phone
without a camera like Jerry Jones, and keep it a few feet from you at all times. If you don't know who's calling you on the phone, let them leave you a message.

Don't trust any PC or the ads you see, question: "Why is that ad showing up now? How does it make me think about myself? If I am being monitored, can the person monitoring me see the same ad, is it supposed to elicit a response in him/her/me?"

Turn off the speakers to your electronics before you go to sleep.

You may feel like attempts at keeping you in poverty will be made. You may "lose" your bank cards and not remember how or when, and eventually you may lose your credit. Keep all paperwork showing you've paid off debts; they sometimes have a way of being "recycled."

Don't claim bankruptcy unless you have no choice, or do anything else that invites a legal investigation.

Try to build a relationship of mutual respect with your local banker, baker, and grocery store clerks. Treat them with dignity. Sometimes a smile from them can change your entire outlook on life. Appreciate every kindness and pray for them, as for your neighbors.

Don't trust the mail—if you're sending something out and can't hand deliver it, mail it certified first-class mail. Get a PO box for mail and package deliveries. Don't take "them" up on free award postcards you receive by mail; there are usually conditions—read the fine print.

Avoid crowds and especially stadiums and theaters. In public places, like restaurants, keep your back against the wall. If you happen to be in public, listen for musical cues in background music. Discern when to use crowds, and random strangers, to your advantage.

You may feel like you are being followed; try not to permit this to unsettle your nerves.

Dress nicely, smell nicely. Do your hair yourself and smile.

If you notice that a nurse prepping you for surgery asks you very specific legal-related questions
while inserting the needle; don't freak out and don't get nervous— your regular doctor isn't in on it.

Don't get plastic surgery or change your name; there really is no place to hide, and you're better off with everyone knowing who you are. Don't forget some people like you; otherwise, there would be no effort to defame and discredit you. *Don't* leave the country.

I once considered throwing myself in the waters off the Florida Keys and hanging on to a piece of wood and claiming I was a boat woman from Cuba just to start over. I hope that gave you a good laugh. Don't bother, they track your every move and as it happens, with the new relations between the USA and Cuba, that is no longer a good "loop hole."

Don't drink from a cup, a can, or a bottle you've left unattended. Sometimes you'll notice the water you drink makes you dehydrated and manic; buy bottled water, and not always in the same place.

Don't frequent any restaurant. Try different places and order different dishes. Change all your filters regularly.

If you notice lights flickering, turn them off and light a flashlight.

Watch your weight and watch for steroids.

Avoid known allergens.

Try to read. Develop your mind. Sometimes a good book is great company. Buy your media (books, DVDs, CDs, newspapers, and magazines) in different stores at different times (try not to mail order them). Discern when to listen to the radio. play video games, or watch TV.

Mow your own lawn. Do your own repairs. Don't let the supposed Jehovah's Witnesses, salesmen/women, or any survey takers in.

Buy a brand-new car and get yourself the extended warranty.

If you notice a helicopter circling your abode or following you as you drive, ignore it. Do not look up at it, do not wave, and do not point at it. And don't think you're doing yourself a favor by taking an IQ test—we're not that smart.

Make something beautiful with your hands, and sell it.

Slow down and smell the wild flowers. Pick out shapes in the clouds. You can bird watch from anywhere. The sound of water falling is lovely.

If someone sings near you, listen to the words (but don't freak out if their words are mocking you, remember the enemy is spiritual); smile, and never mind about the little things.

Give up your weapons, pray instead.

Do not indulge unnecessary blood tests or doctor's visits. Do not donate blood. Pick up your hair clippings when you get a haircut and dispose of them yourself, preferably down the toilet.

If you notice a strange sensation under your skin and your mood being altered, or you're hearing voices, pray.

Don't be surprised if you have a court date and the opposing counsel, a cop, or anyone else looks just like someone with whom you were once very intimate; "they" may want you to know and react to the fact that "they" were watching your intimacies and make you feel like you're being "screwed." Don't react. Remember the person being used might not even know why he/she was selected for the task.

Never mind "their" petty minds; what goes around, comes around, and sometimes letting someone petty and in power have some form of satisfaction could literally save your life. Recognize "their" aim is not to kill you, but to have you damn yourself. Get past it and move on.

Avoid bitterness, allow yourself to feel and to love again in healthy ways. Allow yourself the outlet of crying, but never allow yourself to indulge thoughts of suicide. God gave you life and a cross to carry; carry your cross with dignity and seek Him.

Remember that nothing is impossible for God, have faith. Ask Him for a miracle and to turn things to good. Ask Him for wisdom, calm, and edification for yourself and others.

Remember we sin with our minds and emotions just as much, if not more so, than with our actions. Repent, ask God to forgive you in the name of Jesus. If you haven't yet, acknowledge that
He died for your sins and that He was resurrected in the flesh.

Declare the blood of Jesus over your life and turn it all over to Him. Ask Him to bless you with the Holy Spirit, spiritual gifts, and to guide you.

Unless you're absolutely at your wit's end, don't ask God for divine justice; you might get it, but it's expensive. Remember the word says "Woe to the world for offenses," and though you may feel highly offended at this moment, who knows how many people you've offended.

Don't make vows or offer sacrifices unless you can absolutely fulfill them. God does not require them; we are saved by grace, and everything we have is a gift of God, including our breath.

When you go to church, ask the pastor to pray to break all witchcraft and spells over you and to revoke any and all declarations over you and yours that are not in accordance with His perfect will.

Try to never lie.

Keep a journal and remember to write positive declarations in addition to your fancies, and try to get over it quickly if it goes missing: it may be for the best.

2 FOREWORD

THE GREAT DECEPTION: WAKE UP!

I saw a video last night on Youtube.com about the Illuminati and 2015, and I remembered a lot of things that I'd experienced over the past few years after becoming a Christian and being considered "an enemy of the State, spiritual Babylon."

Before I went to bed, I asked God to give me a dream that I'd remember in the morning, could analyze, and overall for Him to give me understanding and wisdom and guidance, and to not permit Satan to beguile me as to the interpretation: and I asked for this in the name of His son, Jesus Christ of Nazareth. I trust in the Lord, for He is faithful.

This morning I awoke and prayed and received understanding. I looked at the scriptures, in particular Revelation 20 and Revelation 13. And I remembered 1 Corinthians 13:13: "And now abideth faith, hope, charity, these three; but the greatest of these is charity." And I knew, I just knew that part of the Great Deception is the whole issue of the microchip. What if the principalities are programming us Christians to willingly submit to decapitation and death rather than to be microchipped to get us Christians out of the way? And I'm not advising for or against that, many Saints and Prophets submitted to death and in a courageous manner. But think: who in this world right now is beheading whom?

And what if there's no one coming to kill us? What if "they" expect us to kill ourselves when we wake up to the fact that many of us are already microchipped without our knowledge nor consent, or worse: **apostasize** when and if we wake up to the having been implanted with a microchip, or if the rapture doesn't happen during our current understanding of the "Appointed Time" according to many Youtube.com videos which may or not misinterpret the "Appointed Time?" In other words, if "predictions" fail, will many of us feel deceived and will that cause a great falling away of the Church?

Furthermore, what if these existing microchips are vulnerable to viruses, bugs, or identity theft by the enemies of our State and "they" are using these vulnerabilities and the silenced facts about microchips to turn us against each other in this nation?

Though you can't believe everything you see on the news or the internet, I came across an interesting article in the "National Report" citing a study with a lead scientist by the name of John Brugle, Ph.D, which found that 1 in 3 Americans have been implanted with RFID chips, and most are unaware (http://nationalreport.net/study-finds-1-3-americans-implanted-rfid-chips-unaware/). And you can also check out this website: http://www.icaact.org/

And what if we'd had a microchip implanted in us without our knowledge nor consent, then what? What if we already have a microchip? Are we going to lose hope and think we're already damned, Even if the chip isn't on the forehead or the hand?

Read Revelation 20 and 13 carefully. How great is our God? Is He not a supernatural God who fights before His people and who makes the impossible possible? Is He not the God of eternity who sees and knows everything all the time? Do you really think such a plot could escape God Almighty who knows and sees everything on Earth at all times? Of course not, look at the scripture and consider what it says carefully.

In Revelation 20:4-6 we discover that the "SOULS" of the martyrs who'd witnessed Jesus and the word of God, AND which had not worshipped the Beast, NOR his image, NOR had received his mark on their foreheads or in their hands lived (the souls lived) and reigned with Christ a thousand years: that's a lot of conditions. Further, these may be the 144,000 referred to in Revelation 4: 4-6. We are told they (the souls) were blessed and holy and that they are a part of the first resurrection. We also learn later in Revelation 20, that there's a second resurrection of the other dead who will be judged:

> [12] *And I saw the dead, small and great, stand before God; and the books were opened: and another book was opened, which is the book of life: and the dead were judged out of those things which were written in the books, according to their works.*
>
> [13] *And the sea gave up the dead which were in it; and death and hell delivered up the dead which were in them: and they were judged every man according to their works.*
>
> [14] *And death and hell were cast into the lake of fire. This is the second death.*
>
> [15] *And whosoever was not found written in the book of life was cast into the lake of fire.*

(Revelation 20: 12-15 KJV)

But as you see, everyone in the second resurrection will not be cast into the fire. Those raised in the second resurrection do not qualify according to all of the conditions set for the souls resurrected in the first resurrection, but not all will be damned – only those not found written in the book of life!

Now, here's further evidence that the first resurrection has happened. What else does the Bible say about resurrection. First, Jesus was the first to be resurrected in the flesh, and with him others, as evidenced by both Matthew 27: 52-53, and 1 Corinthians 15.

> [50] *Jesus, when he had cried again with a loud voice, yielded up the ghost.*
>
> [51] *And, behold, the veil of the temple was rent in twain from the top to the bottom; and the earth did quake, and the rocks rent;*
>
> [52] ***And the graves were opened; and many bodies of the saints which slept arose,***
>
> [53] ***And came out of the graves after his resurrection, and went into the holy city, and appeared unto many.***
>
> [54] *Now when the centurion, and they that were with him, watching Jesus, saw the earthquake, and those things that were done, they feared greatly, saying, Truly this was the Son of God.*
>
> *(Matthew 27:50-54, KJV)*

In The Word, we also read as Paul explains a mystery of resurrection:

Moreover, brethren, I declare unto you the gospel which I preached unto you, which also ye have received, and wherein ye stand;

2 By which also ye are saved, if ye keep in memory what I preached unto you, unless ye have believed in vain.

3 For I delivered unto you first of all that which I also received, how that ***Christ died for our sins*** *according to the scriptures;*

4 And that ***he was buried, and that he rose again the third day*** *according to the scriptures:*

5 And ***that he was seen*** *of Cephas, then of the twelve:*

6 After that, he was seen of above five hundred brethren at once; ***of whom the greater part remain unto this present, but some are fallen asleep.***

And,

12 Now if Christ be preached that he rose from the dead, how say some among you that there is no resurrection of the dead?

13 But if there be no resurrection of the dead, then is Christ not risen:

14 And if Christ be not risen, then is our preaching vain, and your faith is also vain.

15 Yea, and we are found false witnesses of God; because we have testified of God that he raised up Christ: whom he raised not up, ***if***

so be that the dead rise not.

[16] *For if the dead rise not, then is not Christ raised:*

[17] *And if Christ be not raised, your faith is vain; ye are yet in your sins.*

[18] ***Then they also which are fallen asleep in Christ are perished.***

[19] ***If in this life only we have hope in Christ, we are of all men most miserable.***

[20] ***But now is Christ risen from the dead, and become the firstfruits of them that slept.***

[21] ***For since by man came death, by man came also the resurrection of the dead.***

[22] *For as in Adam all die, even so* ***in Christ shall all be made alive.***

(1 Corinthians 15)

But don't let that stop you from taking Communion. Take heed that no one deceive you (Matthew 24). Remember, Daniel prophesized about the daily sacrifice being taken away and we see a reference to the number of days of the Tribulation in Revelation 12.

[11] *And from the time that the daily sacrifice shall be taken away, and the abomination that maketh desolate set up, there shall be a*

thousand two hundred and ninety days.

(Daniel 12:11)

Also, please note that Ministry itself can be interpreted as the daily sacrifice, because about three and half years was the length of the Lord Jesus' Ministry on Earth: all the more reason to spread the "Good News" of our redemption through the blood and resurrection of our Lord Jesus Christ of Nazareth.

Here's something else to consider, how long is thousand years if a day is like a thousand years to the Lord (2 Peter 3:8), and why are some Pastors referred to as Apostles? Ask the Lord to reveal it to you or ask your Pastor. Consider this also:

This second epistle, beloved, I now write unto you; in both which I stir up your pure minds by way of remembrance:

2 That ye may be mindful of the words which were spoken before by the holy prophets, and of the commandment of us the apostles of the Lord and Saviour:

3 Knowing this first, that there shall come in the last days scoffers, walking after their own lusts,

4 And saying, Where is the promise of his coming? for since the fathers fell asleep, all things continue as they were from the beginning of the creation.

5 For this they willingly are ignorant of, that by the word of God the heavens were of old, and the earth standing out of the water and in the water:

6 Whereby the world that then was, being overflowed with water, perished:

7 But the heavens and the earth, which are now, by the same word are kept in store, reserved unto fire against the day of judgment and perdition of ungodly men.

8 But, beloved, be not ignorant of this one thing, that one day is with the Lord as a thousand years, and a thousand years as one day.

9 The Lord is not slack concerning his promise, as some men count slackness; but is longsuffering to us-ward, not willing that any should perish, but that all should come to repentance.

(2 Peter 3:8, KJV)

This is why it is important to keep worshipping and evangelizing, winning souls for the Kingdom of God, no matter what it looks like out there or what you perceive is occurring in the world.

I remember when I was younger laughing at the saying, "Keep Hope Alive." It's not so funny now. Though Bob Hope has passed, we must still, "Keep hope alive." That's what 1 Corinthians 13:13 above refers to. If you "Google" it, you'll come across some interesting things nowadays, but "Hope," is not just about the Rev. Jesse Jackson, nor the Crystal Method song. Hope is about the hope of Christ, resurrection, and eternal salvation, and it is ours for the asking. Doesn't Jesus Himself say:

27 My sheep hear my voice, and I know them, and they follow me:

28 And I give unto them eternal life; and they shall never perish, ***neither shall any man pluck them out of my hand.***

29 My Father, which gave them me, is greater than all; and no man is able to pluck them out of my Father's hand.

(John 10: 27-29, KJV)

18 Here is wisdom. Let him that hath understanding count ***the number of the beast: for it is the number of a man; and his number is Six hundred threescore and six.***

(Revelation13, KJV)

So, if the number of the beast is the number of a man, does that make the man the beast, or the beast a man? And if you're a man and you are saved, does anything greater than God exist that can "pluck" you out of God's hands? NO. The answer to the second question is a resounding "NO!" If the first resurrection already happened, and the souls lived for a thousand years, and a year may be as a day to the Lord, you may be part of the second resurrection hosting a Born Again soul!

So let's say you were saved and later implanted with a microchip, do you really think you can lose your salvation if you still believe Jesus died for your sins and God raised him from the dead in the flesh three days later and you repent of your sins? Are you that sure you're part of the first resurrection and all those conditions that applied to those Saints apply to you? Or did the first resurrection happen when Jesus rose from his tomb and the bodies of other Saints did too? (See Matthew 27: 52-53, KJV above.) Further, are the souls of the Saints in the first resurrection limited to 1,000 years according to human understanding of 1,000 years, or is there a possibility that could God have other plans? How long is thousand years if a day is like a thousand years to the Lord (2 Peter 3:8).

I once heard a Prophet say, "We live in the clash between two Kingdoms." ("Piercing The Heavens CD," available from Word of Life Ministries, http://www.wolm.net).

Isn't God's word timeless and true, and doesn't The Word say:

> [13] *For whosoever shall call upon the name of the Lord shall be saved.*
>
> *(Romans 10:13)*

So, why fear? Perhaps because the Bible also says:

> [25] *It is enough for the disciple that he be as his master, and the servant as his lord. If they have called the master of the house Beelzebub, how much more shall they call them of his household?*
>
> [26] ***Fear them not therefore: for there is nothing covered, that shall not be revealed; and hid, that shall not be known.***
>
> [27] *What I tell you in darkness, that speak ye in light: and what ye hear in the ear, that preach ye upon the housetops.*
>
> [28] ***And fear not them which kill the body, but are not able to kill the soul: but rather fear him which is able to destroy both soul and body in hell.***

[29] Are not two sparrows sold for a farthing? and one of them shall not fall on the ground without your Father.

[30] But the very hairs of your head are all numbered.

[31] Fear ye not therefore, ye are of more value than many sparrows.

[32] Whosoever therefore shall confess me before men, him will I confess also before my Father which is in heaven.

[33] But whosoever shall deny me before men, him will I also deny before my Father which is in heaven.

(Matthew 10: 25-33, KJV)

Above all, remember 1: Corinthians 6:11. Not one is above reproach (see Ecclesiastes 7:20), but it is the blood of Jesus that redeemed us (see Ephesians 1:7). So, despair not at my recognizing Crystal Method's song, "Keep Hope Alive."

From what did God save me? From what did God save you?

Nevertheless; be wary about whom you pray for, ask God's Spirit for guidance and permission before praying and lay hands suddenly on no one (see 1 Timothy 5:22).

[9] Know ye not that the unrighteous shall not inherit the kingdom of God? Be not deceived: neither fornicators, nor idolaters, nor adulterers, nor effeminate, nor abusers of themselves with mankind,

[10] Nor thieves, nor covetous, nor drunkards, nor revilers, nor

extortioners, shall inherit the kingdom of God.

[11] And such were some of you: but ye are washed, but ye are sanctified, but ye are justified in the name of the Lord Jesus, and by the Spirit of our God.

(1 Corinthians 6: 9-11, KJV)

Now back to the very popular view that whosoever has a microchip will suffer damnation: such videos are all over the internet, you can search for them on Google and on Youtube.com.

I can tell you from personal experience that there is a spiritual battle that occurs within when you realize you may have a microchip. When I realized it, I cried out to God in desperation wondering how He could allow this to happen to me, being a Christian. I was angry at my government and my President. I considered making a vow, though God doesn't require it (Deuteronomy 23: 21-23). I questioned whether or not I had done something horribly wrong against God and if I was being judged: I questioned my salvation until at last I realized that if I was still alive, God must have a purpose in either permitting me to be microchipped (without my consent and without my knowledge), or becoming aware that I had been microchipped. I mourned and experienced what Keebler Ross outlines as the steps of grief: Denial, Anger, Bargaining, Depression and Acceptance.

In time, I learned to recognize when the microchip was activated, sometimes by the sensations I felt in my flesh, sometimes by spots activated in my field of vision, and sometimes by recognizing the thoughts I was having were not normal. Many times, when the microchip was activated it seemed to me as if my beliefs and my faith were under attack, sometimes it presented itself as pure evil all around me, while at others it seemed to be pure evil emitting from me, such as experiencing an overinflated sense of self or deception of being myself divine, or a divine consort, which by God's grace I overcame.

There is also the experience of having your memories be re-written so as to isolate you and break bonds built over time. And I want to tell any reader who is struggling with something like this that there is hope and His name is Jesus Christ of Nazareth. To thwart these types of attacks first submit yourself to Jehova in the name of Jesus Christ of Nazareth, then ask Him to help you resist temptation and to free you and to separate from you anything that may be connected to you illegally and not according to God's perfect will for you by the blood of Jesus. Ask the Lord for mercy and release, and Praise God for his sacrifice and the power of the resurrection. And know that if it doesn't happen immediately, God had a plan and He can turn things to good.

Seek spiritual guidance from your local Christian Pastor. It is so important to go back to God's Word (The Holy Bible), and seek refuge in it: feed your soul and remember Jesus' commandment no matter what you perceive is going on around you (for it may not be occurring in the physical world, but only in your mind and possibly in the spiritual realm. Try to get past the hurt and indignation. Remember, we are grains of sand in time in one Universe - remember God's Word:

> 12 *I, even I, am he that comforteth you: who art thou, that thou shouldest be afraid of a man that shall die, and of the son of man which shall be made as grass;*

[13] And forgettest the LORD thy maker, that hath stretched forth the heavens, and laid the foundations of the earth; and hast feared continually every day because of the fury of the oppressor, as if he were ready to destroy? and where is the fury of the oppressor?
Isaiah 51: 12-13

Remember also Isaiah 54, and above all remember Jesus said:

[27] And he answering said, Thou shalt love the Lord thy God with all thy heart, and with all thy soul, and with all thy strength, and with all thy mind; and thy neighbour as thyself.

(Luke 10:27, KJV)

Nevertheless, if you are not thinking clearly, whether or not you feel you have a microchip, know that it is important to look "presentable" where ever you go. Don't be caught out there looking disheveled if you can avoid it: it makes you vulnerable: try to always wear a smile, believe it or not, it might lighten your mood. You may not always be able to trust your eyes, nor your emotions. Always be praying and asking the Lord to guide you. If you are not experiencing the fruits of the Spirit, recognize something is wrong, isolate yourself temporarily and pray and cast out in the name of Jesus Christ until you do experience His presence:

[22] But the fruit of the Spirit is love, joy, peace, longsuffering, gentleness, goodness, faith,

[23] Meekness, temperance: against such there is no law.

(Galatians 5:22-23, KJV)

Ask the Lord for endurance and patience. Learn to consider your responses and to weigh your words and reactions. Do not despair at those things you experience with your senses. Ask the Lord for discernment and other spiritual gifts available to Christians as outlined in 1 Corinthians 12.

Yes, I've suffered a lot. But I'll tell you something else: despite the distress, God has been there for me every day! And years before the mental and spiritual tribulation which were quite possibly caused when the microchip experiment begun, which was before I became aware of it, God sent me a word of hope and encouragement through a Prophet. I was visiting the town where I spent many of my childhood years in March of 2009, when I decided to attend Church one night and it so happened that the Speaker was a visiting Pastor who was a Prophet I'd never seen before. Towards the end of the service he pointed at me and prophesied: "You! You're going to fight the Giants, and you're going to win! Fight, and you will win." And maybe you can too! Go to church and ask the Lord for a "word."

Frankly, I had no idea who "the Giants," were at that time or what his prophesy could mean. In Genesis 6, we see the Giants are the result of the union of human women and Fallen Angels. And according to the Tom Horn Youtube.com video entitled "Transhumanism and Satan's genetic code," though these Giants were destroyed during the flood from which Noah was spared, their spirits survived and wreak havoc.

Others give different definitions to Giants. Giants can be "Goliaths," or anyone or anything set against you in a spiritual battle. As the following years progressed after that prophesy and I underwent what at times seemed to me like wireless torture, and at others spiritual trials, I held on to the Prophets words for me. I recalled them and I reminded God of the hope he'd sent me with those words, and I took refuge in God's words to me through the Prophet. And I found consolation and deliverance through that promise, for the Lord is not a man that He should lie, and I knew more and more every day that it was the Lord God Almighty who had sent me a word of hope before I even knew I would need it. Just as I knew when He was giving me a Psalm of hope and consolation and later, a calling: I knew those words were meant for me.

Now, I have been a lot of things in my life. And I would be a liar if I didn't admit that at times I backslid. Whether or not it was of my own volition, or whether it was remotely instigated to frame me before the eyes of those monitoring me is no longer important to me. Who's to say if this microchip business is widespread now throughout our nation, and perhaps others, that it isn't some foreign interest trying to turn us in this nation against each other or trying to make certain of us appear dangerous? And yes, perhaps said microchip has the ability to raise our adrenaline levels. But if it does, or for whatever reason you find yourself not enjoying peace and contentment within, perhaps you should pray. For what is important is that the Lord turns all things to good for those who love Him, and I can testify that many times I've asked God to turn negative situations to good, and He has.

> 28 ***And we know that all things work together for good to them that***

love God, to them who are the called according to his purpose.

[29] *For whom he did foreknow, he also did predestinate to be conformed to the image of his Son, that he might be the firstborn among many brethren.*

[30] *Moreover whom he did predestinate, them he also called: and whom he called, them he also justified: and whom he justified, them he also glorified.*

[31] *What shall we then say to these things?* ***If God be for us, who can be against us?***

[32] *He that spared not his own Son, but delivered him up for us all, how shall he not with him also freely give us all things?*

[33] *Who shall lay any thing to the charge of God's elect? It is God that justifieth.*

[34] *Who is he that condemneth? It is Christ that died, yea rather, that is risen again, who is even at the right hand of God, who also maketh intercession for us.*

[35] ***Who shall separate us from the love of Christ? shall tribulation, or distress, or persecution, or famine, or nakedness, or peril, or sword?***

[36] *As it is written, For thy sake we are killed all the day long; we are accounted as sheep for the slaughter.*

[37] *Nay,* ***in all these things we are more than conquerors through him that loved us****.*

38 *For I am persuaded, that* ***neither death, nor life, nor angels, nor principalities, nor powers, nor things present, nor things to come,***

39 ***Nor height, nor depth, nor any other creature, shall be able to separate us from the love of God, which is in Christ Jesus our Lord.***

(Romans 8:28-39, KJV)

So, be encouraged, for The Word says many things about Judgment upon us and upon the Nations, but it also says:

19 *Again I say unto you, That if two of you shall agree on earth as touching any thing that they shall ask, it shall be done for them of my Father which is in heaven.*

20 *For where two or three are gathered together in my name, there am I in the midst of them.*

21 *Then came Peter to him, and said, Lord, how oft shall my brother sin against me, and I forgive him? till seven times?*

22 *Jesus saith unto him, I say not unto thee, Until seven times: but, Until seventy times seven.*

(Matthew 18: 19-22, KJV)

Now be cautious, and pray first that the Lord does not permit you to ask amiss, but know this, Jesus said:

13 *And whatsoever ye shall ask in my name, that will I do, that the Father may be glorified in the Son.*

14 *If ye shall ask any thing in my name, I will do it.*

(John 14: 13-14, KJV)

Now, I am not saying the idea of a microchip is not in itself dangerous, nor am I saying go out and get microchipped: not at all. What I am saying is that if you discover that you or someone you love has been microchipped, keep your eyes and trust in God, feed yourself with the Word and never give up hope that God is greater than anything the enemy can throw against us. Some Youtube.com videos quoting Tom Horn on Transhumanism mention that "they" can change your DNA. Guess what, God can change your DNA too (see Sid Roth's book, Sooner Than You Think).

See Psalm 78 and remember the flesh is temporary, and keep worshiping God Almighty no matter what tries to pull you away from focusing on Him as your Redeemer and your Savior. Do not be afraid to read Psalm 23 and 35 out loud. Be grateful when he sends you a word. Know that every Psalm is truth in worship and that as it refers to in Psalm 50, He is the Judge and Justice of the universe. Remember, Earth is His footstool, and the Lord is our defense.

Here is the text of Jonathan's Cahn's Sapphires E-Mail newsletter that came in as I was writing this Foreword:

King Of The Curse

Friday, August 21, 2015

Matthew 27:29 says that they put a crown of thorns on Messiah. It is a mystery that goes all the way back to Eden. God told Adam and Eve that the ground will bear thorns and thistles as a sign of the world being cursed. Why did they put a crown of thorns on Messiah? They didn't realize that they were declaring Him King of the curse. The crown represents a kingdom, the weight of which rests on the King. The whole weight of the curse rests on Him including our sorrows, our sins and our curses upon Him. He's the king of the curse of the fallen creation. King also means ruler, so He is the Ruler of the curse. That means everything in your life, even the sins, even the consequences, even the bad things, all the thorns in your life; He is Ruler over it and will use it for good. So give thanks for everything, because He wore a crown not of gold to be the Lord of good things, but a crown of thorns to be Lord of all things, especially the thorns of your life.

From Message #1099 - Lord of Eden

Praise God today in your valley of trouble. Praise Him through the trials and bad things happening right now. God is ever faithful to turn these things into good.

Jonathan Cahn is the author of "The Harbinger" and "The Mystery of the Shemitah." His ministry is called "Hope of the World," and may be accessed via this website: http://www.hopeoftheworld.org/ He has revealed many mysteries to the general public in his books and warnings about this year of the Shemitah being from 9/25/14 to 9/13/15. Yes, it could be that private interests have found it beneficial to skew the dates of certain catastrophes to prove Rabbi Cahn wrong. Or it could be that God has decided to show mercy if great calamities do not happen in the USA during this time. So, if additional wide spread calamities or catastrophes don't happen throughout our nation in addition to the Stock Market Crash of "Black Monday" this year on 8/24/15, you may wish to consider either that through not only his warnings, but also through his messages of hope and edification, God could be showing us mercy as many of us simply humbled ourselves and prayed for forgiveness and release from ultimate judgment during this year. Or, you may think that some private interests are trying to discredit Rabbi Cahn. It's your choice how you chose to view it, just keep in mind that God's power is greater and Rabbi Cahn is a servant of the Most High God.

Now, back to the possibility that 1 out of 3 Americans is already microchipped. I will warn you, that one default and effective control mechanism of the microchip is to give your flesh physical pleasure, which can be torturous to some of us and cause others to lose themselves in fornication or other sins of the flesh. Learn to subject your body and pray through it, casting out if necessary and declaring the blood of Jesus over yourself and everyone on the same and surrounding properties. Be cautious as to whom you allow to touch you (see 1 Corinthians 9:27). Try not to fall, but if you do, repent, get back up and fight as soon as you are able: put on Holy Armor and pray.

> *There is therefore now no condemnation to them which are in Christ Jesus, who walk not after the flesh, but after the Spirit.*
>
> 2 *For the law of the Spirit of life in Christ Jesus hath made me free from the law of sin and death.*
>
> 3 *For what the law could not do, in that it was weak through the flesh, God sending his own Son in the likeness of sinful flesh, and for sin, condemned sin in the flesh:*
>
> 4 *That the righteousness of the law might be fulfilled in us, who walk not after the flesh, but after the Spirit.*
>
> 5 *For they that are after the flesh do mind the things of the flesh;*

but they that are after the Spirit the things of the Spirit.

[6] For to be carnally minded is death; but to be spiritually minded is life and peace.

(Romans 8: 1-6, KJV)

Further, if you should experience anger, frustration or depression and question whether or not it is the "mark of the beast", as I did at times, remember Ephesians 6, and also who Daniel worshipped. Remember the conditions for the first resurrection in Revelation 20, received the mark of the beast AND worshipped, etc., and remember that if Jesus didn't return, there should no flesh be saved (see Matthew 24) and pray for revelation and understanding. Remember also this:

[9] And the third angel followed them, saying with a loud voice, ***If any man worship the beast and his image, and receive his mark in his forehead, or in his hand,***

[10] ***The same shall drink of the wine of the wrath of God,*** *which is poured out without mixture into the cup of his indignation; and he shall be tormented with fire and brimstone in the presence of the holy angels, and in the presence of the Lamb:*

[11] And the smoke of their torment ascendeth up for ever and ever: and they have no rest day nor night, who worship the beast and his image, and whosoever receiveth the mark of his name.

[12] Here is the patience of the saints: here are they that keep the ***commandments*** *of God,* ***and the faith of Jesus.***

> [13] *And I heard a voice from heaven saying unto me, Write,* ***Blessed are the dead which die in the Lord from henceforth****: Yea, saith the Spirit, that they may rest from their labours; and their works do follow them.*

(Revelation 4: 9-13)

Do not despair at the mockers, expect them and pray. You may be mocked for believing this and/or for other reasons: it is a tool of the enemy. In 2009 I became convinced that the world would end on 5/12/10. I made preparations. I purchased all types of things that I might need should I survive. I even purchased plane tickets for some loved ones to be with me on that day. The day came and went, and not only did I survive, most others did too and the world did not end. I grew from that experience, but not without some shameful experiences of doubting my faith and backsliding. Whenever I see warnings of "The End of the World" in Youtube.com videos, I remember my experience and not only my own teetering in the faith following it, but also in the credibility I lost among my family. It was a wicked deception, with numerous ramifications. Nevertheless, I always trust in the Lord to turn things to good, and He can. And I have no doubt "The End of the World" is still before us, I simply have hope that if we repent and bring others to repentance we might get a new great revival instead.

Yes, no one knows the day or the hour, but there are signs in the Heavens and there are appointed times on the celestial calendar. Please see Scott Clarke's Eternalrhythmflow's Youtube.com channel; he's predicted that the sign of the Son of Man, akin to the Star of David, may be seen in the Sky in September of 2017. And yes, even our breath is a gift and we need to use our God given discernment to recognize the trials and times we're living in. But I also want to remind you of the Prophet Jonah, the cycles in time and the fall of different Nations and Empires over time.

Not everyone is a Prophet, and not all can understand and accept the lesson in the gourd (see Jonah 4). A disappointment in expectations of the end may lead to a great apostasy or falling away from the Church for those who are not yet mature in their faith, who may consider the warnings themselves a deception and lose faith in their "Shepherds." While some "shepherds" themselves might start to lose faith or courage because they may feel they fell to a deception or lack discernment. Remember to keep your faith in God and to seek His wisdom; to be thankful for everything and try to harness fruitful lessons that you can share from all experiences. God can turn things to good if you just ask Him!

A word about revival and the harvest. Revelation 19 says Jesus is coming back in strength, to rule the nations with a rod of iron, and with the sword proceeding from His mouth. He already died and rose once, and He's left us The Comforter. When he returns, He's coming back with eyes blazing with fire and don't you forget it. He was the sacrifice, He alone was perfect, and the time of His sacrifice is over.

> 11 *And I saw heaven opened, and behold a white horse; and he that sat upon him was called Faithful and True, and in righteousness he doth judge and make war.*

> [12] ***His eyes were as a flame of fire,*** *and on his head were many crowns; and he had a name written, that no man knew, but he himself.*
>
> [13] *And he was clothed with a vesture dipped in blood:* ***and his name is called The Word of God.***
>
> [14] *And the armies which were in heaven followed him upon white horses, clothed in fine linen, white and clean.*
>
> [15] ***And out of his mouth goeth a sharp sword, that with it he should smite the nations: and he shall rule them with a rod of iron: and he treadeth the winepress of the fierceness and wrath of Almighty God.***
>
> [16] *And he hath on his vesture and on his thigh a name written, KING OF KINGS, AND LORD OF LORDS.*
>
> *(Revelation 19: 11-16)*

Our sacrifice according to Hebrews 13 should be to do good, communicate and offer God the praise of our lips: spread the Gospel. He died and rose so that we could have life and have it more abundantly (John 10:10), here on Earth and in the ever after, eternity.

> [15] *By him therefore* ***let us offer the sacrifice of praise to God continually, that is, the fruit of our lips giving thanks to his name.***
>
> [16] ***But to do good and to communicate forget not: for with such sacrifices God is well pleased.***
>
> *(Hebrews 13: 15-16)*

Who would want you to believe that the harvest means letting ourselves be slaughtered instead of bringing more people to the saving knowledge of the grace of Jesus Christ if not those who want to get the Christians out of the way here on Earth? Really. Think about that. Could it be someone who wants to put an end of your life and is looking for an excuse to do so, or for you to do it to yourself or make you "chose your poison/enemy"? Could it be someone who is purposely trying to make you choose your life over your faith? Could it be you're being nudged toward apostasy so that you may lose the favor and protection of God and become vulnerable? It could be for all types of reasons.

Now, those who mind the things of the Spirit and know we'll be alive in Eternity may not be so concerned about our Earthly lives. However, we came forth with a purpose and we received a Commission to spread the Gospel of Jesus Christ, speak boldly, and love not our lives (see Revelation 12). Perhaps if more of us rose up and did this, things just wouldn't look so bleak.

> 18 *And Jesus came and spake unto them, saying, All power is given unto me in heaven and in earth.*
>
> 19 *Go ye therefore, and teach all nations, baptizing them in the name of the Father, and of the Son, and of the Holy Ghost:*
>
> 20 *Teaching them to observe all things whatsoever I have commanded you: and, lo, I am with you always, even unto the end of the world. Amen.*

(Hebrews 13: 18-20)

What if as in Plato's Republic, there is an elite and protected class of "Law Enforcement Officers," in some "New World Order?" What if part of their initiation necessitates taking a microchip? Wouldn't those who call the microchip the mark of the beast be playing right into a sinister plot by not only offending that elite force, which probably has the authority to make your life miserable, but also making them incredibly miserable and doubtful and hopeless by telling them they are damned? Wouldn't you just have played into the true spiritual enemy's hand by causing division, pain and needless despair?

The Word says Woe to the World for offenses. Remember that. And remember you're not the only one who has the right to be offended.

> 7 *Woe unto the world because of offences! for it must needs be that offences come; but woe to that man by whom the offence cometh!*
>
> *(Matthew 18:7)*
>
> 18 *Come now, and let us reason together, saith the LORD: though your sins be as scarlet, they shall be as white as snow; though they be red like crimson, they shall be as wool.*
>
> *(Isaiah 1:18)*

But know this, the Prophets of the Old Testament did not generally give themselves up to be sacrificed. On the contrary, they prayed, raised a borrowed axe from the water while building, and delivered the word of God at great risk while trusting in the Lord God Almighty to deliver them.

How do you fight and win?

On your knees if you are able. This is a spiritual war, it always has been.

[10] Finally, my brethren, be strong in the Lord, and in the power of his might.

[11] Put on the whole armour of God, that ye may be able to stand against the wiles of the devil.

[12] For we wrestle not against flesh and blood, but against principalities, against powers, against the rulers of the darkness of this world, against spiritual wickedness in high places.

[13] Wherefore take unto you the whole armour of God, that ye may be able to withstand in the evil day, and having done all, to stand.

[14] Stand therefore, having your loins girt about with truth, and having on the breastplate of righteousness;

[15] And your feet shod with the preparation of the gospel of peace;

[16] Above all, taking the shield of faith, wherewith ye shall be able to quench all the fiery darts of the wicked.

[17] And take the helmet of salvation, and the sword of the Spirit, which is the word of God:

[18] Praying always with all prayer and supplication in the Spirit, and watching thereunto with all perseverance and supplication for all saints;

(Ephesians 6: 10-18, KJV)

The story of David and Goliath has a meaning in the physical realm and a meaning in the spiritual realm. The meaning in the spiritual realm is closely tied to the meaning in the physical realm. David held five smooth stones and it only took one lodged in the Giant's forehead to defeat the Philistines, remember that. How did God seal the children of Israel? With His Word and the Commandments:

> 16 ***Take heed to yourselves, that your heart be not deceived, and ye turn aside, and serve other gods, and worship them;***
>
> 17 *And* ***then the LORD's wrath be kindled against you, and he shut up the heaven,*** *that there be no rain, and that the land yield not her fruit; and lest ye perish quickly from off the good land which the LORD giveth you.*
>
> 18 ***Therefore shall ye lay up these my words in your heart and in your soul, and bind them for a sign upon your hand, that they may be as frontlets between your eyes.***
>
> 19 *And ye shall teach them your children, speaking of them when thou sittest in thine house, and when thou walkest by the way, when thou liest down, and when thou risest up.*

(Deuteronomy 11: 16-19)

The spiritual interpretation of the story of David and Goliath is to throw the rock of The Word, if it is received, your enemy is sealed and you've done your soul and his or hers, the world and time a great service; if not, move on. Evangelize: in due time if the seed was planted in fertile ground, the fruit will flower (see the parable of the Sower in Matthew 13). If not, your enemy is vanquished. Do not dirty your hands, remember the Commandments and that vengeance is the Lord's.

> [35] *To me belongeth vengeance and recompence; their foot shall slide in due time: for the day of their calamity is at hand, and the things that shall come upon them make haste.*
>
> [43] *Rejoice, O ye nations, with his people: for he will avenge the blood of his servants, and will render vengeance to his adversaries, and will be merciful unto his land, and to his people.*

(Deuteronomy 32: 35-43)

Nevertheless, our Lord is merciful and would rather not one should perish (see Ezekiel 33:11 and 2 Peter 3: 8-10), thus the "Great Commission" given by Jesus Christ to spread the Gospel:

> [14] *Afterward he appeared unto the eleven as they sat at meat, and upbraided them with their unbelief and hardness of heart, because they believed not them which had seen him after he was risen.*
>
> [15] *And he said unto them,* ***Go ye into all the world, and preach the gospel to every creature.***
>
> [16] ***He that believeth and is baptized shall be saved; but he that believeth not shall be damned.***

(Mark 16: 14-16, KJV)

And if you are experiencing less than love for the person to whom you are witnessing, whether it be by speaking face to face to an individual or talking out loud or via EEG to someone, if you find yourself unable to love your neighbor or your enemy from your heart in all honesty, pray and ask the Lord to do it out of His goodness and His heart, with His everlasting knowledge, goodness and wisdom, admitting to God that you are not able to and asking for His will to be done, not necessarily yours. Remember, only God is good (Mark 10:18, KJV), and rest and rely on Him, not on yourself or anyone else. Beg Him for wisdom, temperance and His presence and guidance. Deliver a seed of salvation in hope that it may bare fruit at some time. If it doesn't, at the very least your hands are clean (see Ezekiel 33).

If you're being silenced, do it discreetly. Print personal cards with Romans 10:9 on the reverse side and leave them or hand them out anyplace you are able to. If you use the internet, quote Romans 10:9 whenever you are able to your E-mail list, etc. Give away Bibles. If you like this book, buy a copy for a friend or a fiend, or lend him/her yours. Do a selfless favor for someone else and when they say "thank you," reply, "God bless you." Find a way.

The mark of the beast is a spiritual mark, just as we saw above and again now in Deuteronomy 11:18 that the God's Word is a seal and a mark on the hands and frontlets of the Israelites:

> **_18 Therefore shall ye lay up these my words in your heart and in your soul, and bind them for a sign upon your hand, that they may be as frontlets between your eyes._**

The mark of the beast is the seal of evil and worshiping gods other than Jehova: it is the breaking of the first commandment (see Exodus 20) and rebellion.

Now, just as I am aware of the physical and spiritual aspects of the David and Goliath story, perhaps there is a physical aspect also to the "mark of the beast." Ask the Lord to give you revelation, but also consider the "and, and" conditions and that even if you discover you or someone you care for has a microchip implant, I don't believe it is the mark if you acknowledge and worship God Almighty as your Lord and Savior, repent, and acknowledge that He was raised from the dead in the flesh three days later.

Now, either the Microchip or a virus in the microchip may lead you to dangerous and dark thoughts, but you can overcome them with forgiveness and love and calling upon Jesus Christ of Nazareth – study The Word and pray for healing, forgiveness and personal revelation to come into your heart, especially if you're angry, hurting or have been hurt.

Pastor Gaspar Anastasi at Word of Life Church sent out this blog entry on 8/22/15 and asked the recipients to share it. It was timely, as always:

Unlocking God's Blessings in Your Everyday Life

If you're like me, at times you've wondered in your heart why you haven't seen more of God's blessings manifested in your everyday life. Things like healing, peace of heart, freedom from bad memories and yes, even financial blessings.

I want to share a key I've discovered that is guaranteed to unlock the blessings, starting today. The word of God tells us, His children, that we have been given the keys to lock or unlock blessing from heaven's storeroom (Matthew 18:18). In other words, we could be our own worst enemy because we have locked up our own blessings.

God desires that we release His blessings from His heavenly treasure chests. In spite of what our religious upbringing taught us, we are not waiting for God to release the blessing we so desperately need. He said in Ephesians 1:3 that He has already given us every blessing we need.

So how do we unlock these stored up blessings? Just having the keys is not enough; we must know how to use them to unlock heaven's treasures.

The Bible describes a few keys, but I want to share the one I call the "master key" and give you steps on its correct use. Without this key, God's treasure chest will stay locked up. The master key to unlock every door holding God's blessings is the KEY OF FORGIVENESS!

Use this key and your life will lack nothing. Here is how you start:

Step #1. Make up your mind that forgiving others or yourself is God's will and your purpose in life. The forgiveness that flows out of your life shows the world around you who God really is (He is a forgiving God).

Remind yourself that God forgave all your sins 2,000 years ago.... long before you ever existed! In Matthew 6:9-15, God says forgiveness unlocks heaven's windows so He can pour out His blessings.

Step #2. Turn the key by getting rid of any offense. The moment someone offends you, make sure you're already in the forgiveness mode. Don't wait for them to ask forgiveness but release forgiveness by releasing them from the offense.

Matthew 5:23&24 says, when you're worshipping God, if you remember that someone has something against you, don't wait for them to make it right. Stop what you're doing, go and make it right with them first. Notice how different that is than what today's culture says, which is to wait until they do it first.

Step #3. Turn the key all the way; search your heart for any past un-forgiveness towards someone who hurt or disappointed you, or even towards yourself. Confess that holding un-forgiveness is a sin. We often overlook this sin because it is so acceptable in the body of Christ. We tend to look at the outward, fleshly sins instead of the inward spiritual sins like un-forgiveness.

This master key unlocks the blessings God already purchased for you. By not walking in forgiveness, you lock up God's blessings from being released....blessings like people forgiving you for your wrong!

Have you ever wondered why people seem so unforgiving towards you? It's because the heavens are locked up. Un-forgiveness also locks up the following:

- God's divine favor that opens doors of success.
- God's wisdom to helps you be a good steward over the blessings you do have.
- Healing from a current sickness you have like arthritis, cancer, depression, mental illness, etc.
- Un-forgiveness also blocks the prevention of new sicknesses from attacking you.

It may seem like this master key is difficult to use, but if you are a child of God it's not difficult because God's nature to forgive is inside you.

But, what good is a master key if you never use it? Start using it right now by making a list of people you haven't forgiven. Ask God to forgive you and make a decision to live a life of forgiveness.

Start unlocking your blessing right now. When you ask God for the blessings He promised, expect them to begin to flow because you have the master key. Use it!

Your comments and testimonies are important to us.
Visit our blog page, www.GasparandMichele.com

In addition to forgiveness, hold on to hope. Do not succumb to despair. Know that God is mighty to deliver you, the believer, even when time is tumultuous. Have faith that He will provide. Be encouraged and encourage others; spread the Gospel and message of Salvation.

Appreciate the peace around you, despite what you perceive in your mind. Look out your window, what do you see? I see change. It is true we are still blessed to have windows to look out of and to see houses, buildings and bridges standing, for despite the sometimes necessary protests in our nation, we need to be thankful for our blessings.

Has the USA experienced a devastating Tsunami or reckless and wide spread bombardments throughout our lands? I am not under-estimating the horrible consequences of September 11 or other catastrophes and attacks which have occurred since then. I merely want us to be grateful for the blessing that a "September 11" hasn't physically happened in every town in America Look at the news. Look at what's going on in the world.

Sure, things are not looking quite so beautiful as they once were in the USA, but most of the houses, buildings and our neighbors are still standing, though many are not. Be grateful. Praise the Lord and do as he's asked, bow down and repent for your sins, pray for neighbors, congregate and spread the Gospel of salvation; perhaps He will continue to have mercy upon our nation.

Along with the warnings of the impending physical rapture all over the internet are also warnings about the physical destruction of the USA. As Christians, we must prepare and be thankful for God's mercy should destruction not come and instead of feeling deceived and doubting, we must overcome those thoughts and the perceived mocking and reach thankfulness of God in worship. If we, or some of us, are not raptured and the tribulation in fact begins, be thankful for whatever the Lord decides to fulfill at any given moment: remember, the Earth is His footstool, and the Earth is full of the goodness of the Lord! Be thankful. Be hopeful of God's mercy and undeserved favor. Remember Abraham:

> 18 *Who against hope believed in hope, that he might become the father of many nations, according to that which was spoken, So shall thy seed be.*

(Romans 4:18, KJV)

I acknowledge that many believe judgment is overdue; however, consider the first verse of Psalm 136:

> *O give thanks unto the LORD; for he is good: for his mercy endureth for ever.*

(Psalm 136, KJV)

Repent, and let others know that while they are alive, they still have the opportunity to come to repentance and be saved by Grace.

The Pastor at Word of Life church said in the 8/23/15 service:

"Your worst enemy isn't the Devil, it's your mouth."

Look at what James 3 says:

> *My brethren, be not many masters, knowing that we shall receive the greater condemnation.*
>
> 2 ***For in many things we offend all. If any man offend not in word, the same is a perfect man, and able also to bridle the whole body.***
>
> 3 *Behold, we put bits in the horses' mouths, that they may obey us; and we turn about their whole body.*
>
> 4 *Behold also the ships, which though they be so great, and are driven of fierce winds, yet are they turned about with a very small helm, whithersoever the governor listeth.*
>
> 5 ***Even so the tongue is a little member, and boasteth great things. Behold, how great a matter a little fire kindleth!***
>
> 6 ***And the tongue is a fire, a world of iniquity: so is the tongue among our members, that it defileth the whole body, and setteth on fire the course of nature; and it is set on fire of hell.***
>
> 7 *For every kind of beasts, and of birds, and of serpents, and of things in the sea, is tamed, and hath been tamed of mankind:*

8 *But the tongue can no man tame; it is an unruly evil, full of deadly poison.*

9 *Therewith bless we God, even the Father; and therewith curse we* ***men, which are made after the similitude of God***.

10 *Out of the same mouth proceedeth blessing and cursing. My brethren, these things ought not so to be.*

11 *Doth a fountain send forth at the same place sweet water and bitter?*

12 *Can the fig tree, my brethren, bear olive berries? either a vine, figs? so can no fountain both yield salt water and fresh.*

13 *Who is a wise man and endued with knowledge among you? let him shew out of a good conversation his works with meekness of wisdom.*

14 *But if ye have bitter envying and strife in your hearts, glory not, and lie not against the truth.*

15 *This wisdom descendeth not from above, but is earthly, sensual, devilish.*

16 *For where envying and strife is, there is confusion and every evil work.*

17 *But the wisdom that is from above is first pure, then peaceable, gentle, and easy to be intreated, full of mercy and good fruits, without partiality, and without hypocrisy.*

[18] And the fruit of righteousness is sown in peace of them that make peace.

(James 3: 1-18, KJV)

Notice in James 3:9 it says that men are made in the similitude of God. In many verses in the Bible we are referred to as Sons of God! Do you know the power of creation and declaration? Do you know what Rhema is? In Strong's concordance it means "to cast or throw," just as in the spiritual interpretation of the David and Goliath (1 Samuel 17) story mentioned above, declaring a word has power: start declaring good; for all you know, a word you throw can defeat and simultaneously save a "Giant" by winning him/her over to the Kingdom of God!

Well, what if you're not a believer? Google Sedona Effect and choose this website: http://sedonanomalies.weebly.com/ Ben Lonetree has several eye opening articles about the effect of human consciousness and brainwaves being in sync with our environment. Are we going to sit idly by and not even try to be more than passive bystanders on Earth as emotions, behaviors, weathers and rumors of war run amock, or are we going to use our human energy to push out waves and pulses of love into the Universe?

Some "New Agers" or science fiction fans you may know might call this "Cosmic Balance," frankly, I don't know enough about it to be sure. However the term brings to my mind both Genesis 1 and Isaiah 45. God created light from darkness and God creates good and evil, He even created the smith, as evidenced in Isaiah 54. Learn to tip the balance back to "Good." Apostle says Christians are called to be as lights:

13 For it is God which worketh in you both to will and to do of his good pleasure.

14 Do all things without murmurings and disputings:

15 That ye may be blameless and harmless, the sons of God, without rebuke, in the midst of a crooked and perverse nation, among whom ye shine as lights in the world;

16 Holding forth the word of life; that I may rejoice in the day of Christ, that I have not run in vain, neither laboured in vain.

(Phillipians 2: 13-16, KJV)

For Christians, among other things, this could mean honor God and Jesus Christ: spread the Gospel whether or not you have or believe you have a microchip! Remember God has sealed your hand and your frontlets with his Word (Deuteronomy 11), and His laws are written in your heart:

3 Forasmuch as ye are manifestly declared to be the epistle of Christ ministered by us, written not with ink, but with the Spirit of the living God; not in tables of stone, but in fleshy tables of the heart.

(2 Corinthians 3:3, KJV)

For non-Christians it may mean, focus on the positive. Seek faith, hope and love.

Another aspect of what many Christians call these end times for non-Christians is the correlating view held by many scientists resting on visible evidence, interpreted in different ways, of things we see occurring on Earth at this time. For some of us, we consider the "Illuminati, or the New World Order" the threat. While others may have read Elizabeth Kolbert's The Sixth Extinction, or seen one of many popular movies or music videos warning about the end of our era. Perhaps we should be asking, "Has it happened before, and has God left a Remnant?, Has Revival come and gone, or can it come again?"

Could it be we are opening "Gateways," with our words, declarations and Remah, or is it truly the end of Earth as we know it? Have we passed the "Point of No Return," and will there be a remnant? Is there still time to humble ourselves before God Almighty and seek miracles? Or have we come to "Judgment Day?" And if so, did we bring it on ourselves out of ignorance, division, sin and lack of humility?

Lastly, I want to address another technological possibility which may seem like science fiction to some of you. We all know there there are clouds in the sky, and "cloud servers for data." What if as part or in addition to the microchip situation, there were to exist a "consciousness database?"

This is where I need both Christians and Non-Christians to think of balance. In particular the balance of good and evil in included or uploaded consciousness. This is where I believe faith, a positive and forgiving attitude could make a great impact if "The Consciousness Cloud" is to become a wide-spread reality and we are not given a choice as to whether or not we are going to accept it.

Remain calm. It could be just a hypothesis, but if God has permitted it to exist, it is His choice when and if to terminate it. What we need to focus on is our own principles and not compromising that God has called Christians to be lights in the midst of darkness and remain positive and forgiving.

There are Christian Servants and there are Christian Cleaners, and most of our work occurs in the spiritual realm, while we pray. If you are feeling overwhelmed by consciousness, take courage. Pray, take authority in the name of Jesus Christ of Nazareth. Consider the microchip that may or may not be in you and ask the Lord to somehow turn the situation to good. Evangelize. Reverse hack it. Edify the consciousness of its central command. Be led by the Spirit. Minister. Offer Romans 10:9, multiply and forgive. Then praise the Lord for where he's put you at any given moment.

Life is more complex than anyone really needs to know: just live, love, laugh, forgive and share the fruits of the Spirit in your prayer and meditations. Perhaps the Lord will show us Mercy.

> 22 *But the fruit of the Spirit is love, joy, peace, longsuffering, gentleness, goodness, faith,*
>
> 23 *Meekness, temperance: against such there is no law.*
>
> *(Galatians 5: 22-23, KJV)*

3 SCRIPTURE I

Wash you, make you clean; put away the evil of your doings from before mine eyes; cease to do evil; Learn to do well; seek judgment, relieve the oppressed, judge the fatherless, plead for the widow. Come now, and let us reason together, saith the Lord: though your sins be as scarlet, they shall be as white as snow; though they be red like crimson, they shall be as wool. If ye be willing and obedient, ye shall eat the good of the land: But if ye refuse and rebel, ye shall be devoured with the sword: for the mouth of the Lord hath spoken it.

(Isaiah 1: 16 - 20, KJV)

4 ACKNOWLEDGMENTS

First and foremost, I want to thank God for his unending mercy and faithfulness. I also want to thank my family members for their patience and support.

I want to thank Gladys Deliz of Puerto Rico, for taking me to Pastor Ramon's church as a child. And I want to thank Mother Jean for finding a lost sheep, and returning her to the fold. I want to thank each pastor and brother and sister in Christ who has prayed for me and my family (or who will), as well as my Educators, Mentors, previous employers and Counselors.

In particular, I want to express sincere appreciation to: Gumersinda Velez, Andres, Angelique, Mark, Natalie, Anastashya, Adrian, Jesus and Migdalia Andujar and also Emily Forti and Jennifer Herrera-Andujar (family members who put up with me when no one else would!). A love note to my aunts, uncles, cousins and grandmother, Felicita Mercado Febo, for always being there for me! A note of tender memories to David Matt Wright and Alan Ladd Clem and their families. The scent of a fresh bouquet of flowers in appreciation to Bill and Jill Roberts, Colleen Moynihan from NEBA's Ticket-to-Work program, John B. Hoffman— founder of the Albert G. Oliver Program (now known as Oliver Scholars Program in NYC), and to the numerous, unseen and seen, imagined or not, "associates" and "assets" throughout my life.

I also want to thank those who've provided excellent medical care to me; in particular, Ms. Delpizzo, Dr.Grendys and staff, Dr. Hart and staff, Dr. Machlin and staff, Ms. Angela Monterosso, Dr. Mehta, Dr. Tritel and staff (especially Nurse Patty Minalga), Dr. Webb and staff, and Dr. Yamashita and staff. I also want to thank Martha S. Horton, my psychologist throughout college, for acknowledging me and declaring good over me in her book, Seashell People. And though I don't remember her name (please forgive me), I had a terrific psychologist during high school who taught me the importance of having options.

Thank you to my friends and neighbors (especially Ingrid, Irene, Johanny and Joan), fellow Christians, and patient Pastors especially those from Word of Life Ministries (WOLM.NET), Camino a Salvacion Church, Ministerio Nueva Esperanza (http://www.ministerionuevaesperanza.com/web/), and Iglesia Vida Cristiana in Cape Coral. I also want to thank numerous online Ministries for their timely and freely shared information including Trunews.com, Sidroth.org, Erfministries.com, Openyoureyespeople.com, Hopeoftheworld.com, Sonlifetv.com, and Joyce Myers and Ambassador Juanita Bynum for their powerful telecasts on Youtube.com.

Also a special note of thanks to Professor Larry Udell Fike, author of "Piker" for his faithful and selfless friendship, before and after I became a Christian. Larry, I don't agree 100% with your recollection of me on the train back in the 1990's as recounted in

"Piker," but I'm glad I found you again and for your continued friendship and acceptance of my changes and growth. And a shout out in appreciation for friendship to Regina Winters who gave me my first journal, Tara Chambers for telling me about Xango while I was getting chemotherapy and Tina Clark for my ability to remember her smiling calmly and safely no matter what was going on, also to Natalie Barlow for keeping me in the loop, and to Kenny Tate for great Facebook posts! And I also want to thank the marketers of Deep Sea Cosmetics in Port Charlotte and Fort Myers for making their wonderful lotions affordable to me: Mazel Tov!

Yes, I also want to thank Uncle Sam. It is true that there is no better country than the USA. I haven't been to a lot of places, but I watch the news. I see what's going on around the world, and no matter what I'm going through, imaginary or not, I thank the Lord that I was born a US citizen. I know Uncle Sam's not perfect, but neither am I—or you, for that matter. So whether you discover you're a "rabbit" or that you're "asleep" or "awake," keep in mind our uncle is family and help to edify him— soon enough all will be okay. Also remember: "One Nation Under God," and the threats against this nation both from within and without; appreciate peace and love thy neighbor.

Lastly, I want to thank the nameless, faceless, imaginary or real, spooks, and the ones whose faces I got to see. Yes, believe it or not, I would not be healing without you. God turns all things to good! I want you to know that I recognize you too are oftentimes trapped by your circumstances and need to survive. I know the burden of the knowledge you hold is great, and I know that many of you are redeemed, and I will continue to pray that many more of you are too, for the sake of your souls and for the sake of our country.

This compilation of poems is rolled out as one long poem which spans the journey of the spiritual growth of an adulterous woman in a nation spinning, while facing unspeakable adversity with grace and love. It also deals with individual spiritual growth and transferring love from a man to God, and also with National Politics in the USA and the threat of ISIS. It was written as poetry, but I would love to hear it as "Spoken Word Poem" and welcome offers to record this long poem in the Spoken Word artform, please see the About the Author page for contact information.

Dearest friends, for a long time I was in a place where my exterior circumstances controlled me internally, and I was miserable, not only because it wasn't I who had control, but also because those external circumstances were being imposed against my will, and like many others, I blamed it on our President in my poetry (reminds me of Pink's song, "Mr. President," which was for George W. Bush's Administration).

Eventually, I started opening my mind to the possibility that if the good Lord had permitted so and so to happen, despite intercessory prayer, there was a reason for it and it was His Will. I still didn't like it; so, He opened up the heavens and showed me a little piece of His masterpiece here on earth- He let me see the grid and bad stuff too. Then I realized, I'm just a little spec of sand on the map of time, in one universe, and if I could do some good to at least one other little spec of sand or two – that would probably be enough, and if there was some way the good Lord could use even my suffering and frustration, He would use it for at least my own benefit and someone else's. God is great and nothing is wasted! So no matter what you're going through, know that God will somehow turn it to good in due time. Relish the fight! But love will get you peace.

Blessings, hugs and warm thoughts to you and yours!

God bless us and God bless the USA!

-Audrey Andujar Wright

5 ABOUT THE AUTHOR

Audrey Andujar Wright is a New York City native who was brought up in the East Coast and Puerto Rico. Her cat's name is "Terror Wright."

At age fifteen, she became an Albert G. Oliver Scholar and was placed at George School, a Quaker Boarding School in Pennsylvania, where she started to keep journals.

She was a Dyckman Scholar while at Columbia University in New York, from where she graduated in 1992 with a bachelor's degree in Comparative Literature. Audrey worked at various Fortune 500 companies as well as the State of Florida through 2009, where she was a Certified Project Manager Professional at the time, serving as Assistant Director of District Management for the Florida Department of Environmental Protection.

Audrey was diagnosed as Bipolar in 1997: despite the diagnosis, she was able to enjoy a successful career in Public Service - however, things changed when she was also diagnosed with Cancer in 2009.
Thankfully, as of August 2015, Audrey is in remission (Bless the Lord!).

In addition and like many of you, Audrey has suffered job loss and foreclosure. If you'd like to help Audrey monetarily, please send a check to her via return receipt, certified mail to: P O Box 762, Fort Myers, FL 33902-0762 or via Paypal to Audreywright1@msn.com.

Audrey welcomes correspondence and reserves the right to publish any and all of it. You may view Audrey's LinkedIn Profile at: https://www.linkedin.com/pub/audrey-wright/7/48/3a8 . You may wish to periodically view her websites to check for new content: http://theheal.info http://www.audreyandujarwright.com, and http://www.mypeopleperishforlackofknowledge.com .

6 MY TESTIMONY

In 2009, I was a well-compensated professional, making over $100,000 a year with benefits in State government. I'd worked in the private industry for years before that, starting a summer job as a Directory Assistance Operator at New York Telephone Company at age 14 while an Albert G. Oliver Program Scholar, attending George School, a private Quaker boarding school in Pennsylvania where I'd been granted a scholarship. In fact, I worked before that. I can remember operating a cash register at the tender age of six years old, while regularly helping out my Dad in his Grocery Store across the street from the elementary school where we lived in Puerto Rico at the time. And I had managed to help my sister, and mother relocate to Florida, find housing and employment in 2006 when the economy started sliding in Puerto Rico, where they lived at the time.

By 2009, I had a great career, family, friends, a husband, a house, a car, two cats, and I got along with my boss. I'd figured out the way for me to get ahead was to keep promoting upward every couple of years, even if it meant transfers. I felt accomplished, confident, sexy and unstoppable!

Then I got sick. Really, it's that simple. What changed my life initially was the dual diagnosis of Ovarian and Uterine Cancers. Because though I had been diagnosed bipolar in 1997, I was on meds and got promoted every couple of years consistently. I had earned two commendations from Governor Bush in 2001 for successful suggestions to save the State of Florida money in addition to numerous Davis

Awards, and I had earned a degree from Columbia University in the 1990's: in my mind, I was set.

And then, my world changed. In 2007 I began experiencing serious health problems and by 2008 I had scheduled a hysterectomy to avoid any related problems from interfering with my career. But God had other plans. Isn't God marvelous!

Eventually I realized and recognized that the priorities in which I'd based my feelings of accomplishment were not as they should have been, and I changed; but not without first experiencing personal tribulation that led to growth, and the emotional maturity which I had lacked when I was first Born-Again. And I received an education much more precious than my Ivy League Degree and Project Manager Professional Designation that I'd enjoyed while employed.

Today, I seek and enjoy His Presence, knowing growth is continual and so looking forward to new lessons and the impartations received through prayer. And I enjoy writing as a hobby, which I have done since I was fifteen years old.

A large part of my testimony is laid out in the poem, "Oh Love," which follows this chapter and I hope you'll enjoy it. If you'd like to hear more details of my testimony, invite me to your Church where I can share not only my testimony, but also my writing with the congregation; and thank you for considering me: See the About the Author Page, audreywright1@msn.com or 239-989-4579 (AT+T).

7 OH LOVE

"Attend to my precepts, then, you disappointed gallants,
All those whom their loves have utterly betrayed.
Let him who taught you to love now teach you love's cure-
Take succor from the hand that struck the wound!
Don't let your heart be enslaved To its particular vice."
(Ovid, "The Cure for Love," The Amores)

Oh Love…

I felt him yesterday, he is like champagne.

And he spoke to me: he could feel my pain.

In him there was no feeling of disdain

And no, he's not truly that vain.

I didn't expect it, I was afraid

And I pulled back right away

But he'd been waiting for me, I could tell.

He was even prepared to share the pain.

He's not self-righteous

Yet liberties he will take

He's 100% man, nothing fake

If only I could see his face.

He's tender, patient and kind

And he gives hugs, but most of all

He's a man and he's in control.

Undying love for me he will feign

So long as I don't alter his pace.

For true friendship is what awaits

Across the finish line in this race.

I can sense his smile bubble up

And it's contagious for our friends -

Patience, love, charity all the way

That's a gift I can now take.

And in return I will try

To keep stable this mind of mine

And bring not down into the brine

The mind that settles my own mind.

Can you see past this flesh?

Can you light the bud in my heart?

Do you feel it swelling within?

Does it touch you the way it does me?

When you listen to the music

Do you remember feelings from afar?

Things experienced but not felt?

No. No touching or we'd melt.

Being in love, yet not knowing when

Somewhere in time, I'd call you on a dime.

Yes "those were the days,"

Still some would say.

And yet there is too much

For these eyes to betray.

In age they grow weak

And our skin's now frail.

Just as in those days

When from afar we'd feel,

So it must be now

When we are oh so aged.

'Tis age that separates us now

No longer miles apart

Or held back by wedding bands.

Oh "Adulteress" you scream!

And yet my love ran so deep

For both my husband and my friend.

Though touch the latter I never did,

Lest you consider holding a hand.

Sometimes beneficial it is

To have somebody to get dressed up for

Makes life all the more interesting

And you stop wandering what it's all for,

Or so I thought during that time.

A little love interest

Can brighten your day

As long as you don't

Jump in the hay!

But adultery is adultery.

No let us not forget.

What is in our heart

Is what our heart begets.

You must think I'm really weird,

But you see you represent

A whole garden of professionals

I've learned to trust as friends.

Though they have bosses that abhor me,

And sometimes even them

God always knows what He's doing,

And sometimes He's prodding them.

Yes I know you sometimes call her Hen

Even if her name is Jen.

Don't let her catch you reading this:

It's not meant for Jen or Ben.

Yes I know all about Ben

Or at least I think I do

With his evil machinations

Casting spells all over this nation.

And yet would you believe

I've even prayed for him too?

Believe it if you will

I can't deny it's true.

I felt him growing ill

And prayed in intercession

And I think God actually

Unhardened Ben's heart

Toward you and toward me.

Isn't that a miracle?

I hope He healed him too.

As much as possible

Even if just to show

He has the power to do so.

So now back to you and me.

Mr. Prism you are to me.

Whether or not you know it

Or not…

Whether or not you are.

The guys behind the glass

They do monitor our E-mails

And sometimes help us out

Yes! Isn't that just grand?

Well I was praying tonight

And you know what came to me?

I should ask for proof of life.

Are you sure you're still in this realm Gene?

Can I access you here too?

I know I heard you loud and clear

At a completely different level,

But then your voice it went away.

Are you still here on this earth?

Do you share the air with me?

When I look into the sky at night

Can I vector into you in bounce

Or does it actually transcend

Into the hidden realms?

Proof of life is what I want

No prism jokes, no prison laughs

Won't you please provide it please?

Think of Mendel and the peas,

And deny not this mutant still.

And just in case you doubted it

Here is proof that I Bipolar am

As I sat down to think

And reverie about my poem

I thought what a piece of dirt you are.

To have embroiled me in some fantasies

No it was not only one.

To get my mind all twisted up

In things I never dared imagine

Could exist, even perhaps.

This new movie coming out

Eight senses or something like that

That shit's real Gene

And it is not only spiritual

It's an AI perversion

Of the most wicked type.

It's the new consternation

The Matrix new and hyped.

They layer us once activated

To make us seem insane

In some hell-hole you will find them

Perhaps at the end of time

Unless they soon repent.

If you must know our population

Is vulnerable to attacks and hacks

Not only foreign, but also from "out back."

I won't name them, what's the use
Just as evil exists, good does too.

Yet I'm grateful for some semblance
Of me back to who I was,
Just today I spent some time
Remembering how it was.

You wicked thing
Why'd you have to go
Take so much innocence from me?

Sometimes it's better not to know
The why, the who, the when and where.
I suppose I had some part in it,
By falling into the snare.

You were irresistible then

And sometimes you still are,

But only if I get some proof of life:

Do you accept the dare?

Oh, how I envy thy flesh,

So taught and rosy,

Embracing your very being,

Penetrating the crude depths

Of both your soul and mind.

So torturous to know

That mine could never come so close

To your essence.

That this union can never

Fully bind us forever as one!

Oh hatred, what has thou done?

I held you close to my heart,

For Oh so long;

But many years it has been

Since you fondled me

And I cooed at your embrace.

Like a lover

You creep in unannounced

You steal a smile

And turn it around

Into a frown.

Self-important laughter you cajole.

You make me chuckle with delight.

You dole out delusions

Disguised in light.

You fondle the hem of my skirt

Running your hands over my breasts

So close, my heart you penetrate.

You whisper in my ears

Inaudible tirades;

And yet make your impression felt

As palpable as your black breath.

Must I succumb to you?

Today of all days?

Easter Sunday in the USA?

"How does he live with himself?"

You instigate,

Mocking indignation

Just below your breath.

"How does he feel when he's alone?"

In an attempt to fish out sympathy

And place yourself on the throne

Of my heart, yes, all alone.

My tears, they will not come.

Oh Hatred, what hast thou done?

You've dealt me a mortal blow

In trying to turn my heart to stone.

You don't know how I've longed

For you to be free of your Office.

For me to never have been discovered

For us to have met at

A different time, a different place;

In a reality foreign

To this, my living hell.

A poor excuse for a Christian I am

But a Christian all the same.

I turn this over to You Lord

Before I go insane.

I'll take a pill. I'll be Okay.

As your friends grin

And shout "Hurray."

A woman scorned

You've managed to make

All alone, putrid with hate.

Why do I feel

This great heaviness in my heart?

Why this choking,

Why in my throat this knot?

This wrestling at my soul

Why do these tears well up?

For good has he now gone?

For who's good? Mine? Not.

Though he rejected me incessantly,

I couldn't help but love him earnestly:

He was my soul mate and my friend.

Though perhaps to him I was just a fiend.

And so life goes on without him.

How did he get to be where he was?

Who gave him access into my home?

And who has now taken him away

From me?

Where do I get this capacity to love –

Love in captivity and love when free

And why does my heart still yearn for him?

O, where could he be?

Has God gathered him up to Him?

Does he move among the Angels?

O, where could he be?

So long and so frequent

I've prayed the Lord

Break this spirit tie please

If it His will it be,

But perhaps it is not

And won't be 'till I die.

Is my love hurt, is he injured?

Has evil touched or molested him?

Has he been made to sin?

What ails him? Who hurt him?

Alas, I cannot know

But pray for him I must.

What ails my beloved

Is it a family member he's lost?

Or indeed another love?

What pulls at his heart

So hard that I can feel it too?

Though we're miles apart.

Why does his soul angst aghast

What is his fate? Alas,

Why are we separated by war?

Revive him Lord I pray.

Cost me what it may.

Oh let the Holy Spirit descend

And comfort him and comfort me

And comfort them,

In Jesus' name I pray.

As burning lava once flowed

On Mount Olympus,

I feel your love run over me wholly

Perhaps it was, perhaps it wasn't

You, Oh Lord, who ruled back there.

Of you I beg greater understanding, Sir.

Enlighten my little mind I plead,

For it is you I seek to please

Fulfill me with your secret mysteries

Known to few in your eternity.

Your thunder it does answer me.

Is it a warning that I hear?

A cycle with a twist restoring

A new era, the reign of "she"?

Though in the midst

Of the beginning of sorrows

I find myself to be,

Thy will be done in me

Lord, help me please

I beg of thee

Don't let arrive

Those things I see.

In intercession you founded me.

Now let them see

It's peace I seek.

Salvation means eternity.

I heard you called me an ingrate.

Beware, they're trying to make you hate

That little project you once called "X."

If you would turn off your TV,

The IPOD, the radio, and the PC

Soon enough you'd start to see

Yourself thinking naturally.

If you'd think clearly you'd realize,

I know that at times you were kind

Oh no, don't you now get confused

It is not of the beast I speak

But actually of the PSYOPS Police.

It was with kindness you devised

Slow jams, music for my rides.

They were intercessions you would hide

While making me want to get high.

A populace asleep this season

Were you orders without reason,

And how could you not behest

When they threatened you with treason,

And you'd seen them Saints behead.

Oh friend I am not mad at you

If you must know, I pitied you

That's why I made every attempt

For seeds to plant so you'd be saved.

When this all started I'd had a dream

That though I didn't understand

I knew my job was to prevent

Souls being lost; that I'd regret.

My sister, now desolate, barren and black

I too have been betrayed by that man, Barack

To my face he feigned a smile

Followed by the wiping away

Of imaginary tears

As if I wouldn't, as if I couldn't

See the only cross about him

Were his fingers crossed

Behind his back.

My sister, the tears you have held back
Don't let them corrode you from the inside
Don't let "The Man" wield that axe
That can pollute you deep inside
And poison on the outside,
The opposite of the Midas touch,
He can make
What you touch turn awry.

Forgive me my sister if I seem vulgar
But there is no other way to describe
The hurt "The Man" will try to unleash
On your remaining, now famous, family

Wicked, unholy contortions they will plot
And in sins they will attempt to entrap

With things as simple as the jingle

Of a song advertising ice cream

That may as well be selling crack.

My sister, don't be fooled

For the world is now dark

The TV is riddled with PSYOPS

While supposed great Mayors

Hide atrocities behind arguments

For soda pop.

My sister don't be blinded

Tribulation is upon us;

Upon you and upon me.

There is no rhyme or reason

For our President's treason

Of his own family.

For that is how he sold it to us
"We are family," lest we forget
But there's no more Sister Sledge
In this new era, there's a new jingle
One you and I have not yet heard.
It is full of drum beats and crescendos
While a melodic chorus pulls at your heart strings
Yes sister, there is a new song
For your hurt they'll try to cover up.

They make you naked and send you into battle
With remote cameras they watch on saddles
Snacking as they feast their eyes,
Feigning shock and making faces at their friends
While they watch the beasts tear apart your flesh.

O sister, do not be fooled

The days when all it took

Was a jester to entertain

Are long past overdue.

The times are now wicked, unholy; perverse

And few are left who haven't transgressed

Do yourself a favor and accept

The one true light that still remains

Like CeCe Wyans said,

His name is Jesus.

Now I know that doesn't rhyme.

Perhaps discordance it will symbolize

For once you accept Him, your world will change.

Yeah, your entire existence will cease to be the same.

Yes sister, it is true,

Life more abundantly you will see and have

Even treasures of darkness you may yet have

Dominion over serpents and scorpions, His gift to you

But in these times, be prepared, for you may discern

The scorpions, the serpents,

And rodents too close to you.

So do not make the decision lightly.

We all know some of us are lively

And the senseless, fickle caprices

Of our flesh we'll need to shed.

And yet sister, I can tell you

The walk is worth it,

For eternity you will gain.

And not just eternity,

But a faithful friend:

Someone who will listen

And talk back to you gently

Someone who won't judge you

Without a gentle correction

Someone who will care

To polish your very heart

Someone who will love it,

Even if it's black.

Cast your cares on Him, not on Barack

We all know who really has the power

To mend ills and give us justice and grace

both in the Heavens

And on the Earth.

Although a pilgrim I am not,

You need not have sailed on the Mayflower

For your blood to boil so hot

Upon the crumbling of our towers.

“But you lived in Florida at the time”

You protest; yet a “cracker” I am not.

Oh don’t get all bent out of shape.

It’s an expression I once heard.

To be truthful you could not find

A Rican more Republican than I.

Though I must not hesitate

To tell the truth about my trance;

For Obama I did vote once

And a witness I do have,

In case they try my truth to trash.

Browsing the net I did peruse

A beautiful picture of the GW Bridge

It was arraigned red, white and blue

A large, majestic flag hung from a beam
Oh what a shame that it would be
If it were not made in the USA.

Won't someone please investigate
To whom give credit for that create.

Yes, things have changed horrendously
Since I watched the strike on the TV
In my Palm Bay home I was
On the phone with family.
For my brother he still lived
In the Bronx, oh at Auntie's
Not too far from where an old friend
Sheena's mom once gave me "greens."

Forgive me please if I digress
Full disclosure is not my intent.

The problem is I've come to learn

No longer is there privacy.

We acted swiftly when in shock

When that great terror our Towers struck.

Oh, not just in our families

Throughout the land angst in our souls.

We all felt that "Monster Truck."

And now that "Monster" is a front

For things we dare not even speak.

Coded PSYOPS you do drink

It's on the billboards and TV's.

Perhaps you heard the CDC

Mention something about Zombies.

But as if that were not enough,

Abused has been even the glove

That once fit so perfectly

On Jesse Owens in '36.

Oh friends don't let the colors blind you

For the terror is right beside you

It hides behind a teleprompter

And a great, big family.

Some of whom have tried to turn us

Into Transhumans and Zombies

Now I did not always know.

Don't forget for him I've prayed

And yes, also for his family.

Though he would not want you to know it

No, "The Man" has hid my name

"Audrey Andujar or Audrey Wright"

In that "Secret Bill" he kept.

"Redrum, Murder!" I decry

For the cover up is so sublime

It may just blow away your mind.

They were counting on my mimes

Didn't think I had a mind

Capable of recovery.

From the fury leashed upon me

NSA cars still do stalk me

By a beast and other friends

He attended college with

And sometimes refers to as "family."

"Mr. President, you've crossed the line

You yourself said had been set

Against killing your own peeps."

Death panels do now exist

You must by now have noticed

If you get Medicaid, SSI or SSD.

And when they're not sufficient

To empower them to finish

Certain "Poet Pests" like me

They send some people out "To Fish."

And when the Lord, He intercedes

Protecting my whole family,

A little nation is quickly targeted

And in the Bill my name interred

As if I were a Terrorist.

Freedom of Speech no that is gone

Wake up to this reality.

Brother, sister the time has come

For this President to impeach,

For if you still like me believe

Time to heal there might still be!

Sometimes Evil itself

Will tempt you with a kingdom

When you're so close to achieving it

Simply by following your principles.

The Gospel of Peace is not

The "Go Spell of Pieces" or Pisces:

Every word is true and timeless

Unite efforts instead:

Pervail instead of behead

Or do you want to be perceived as ISIS

Do you want to win the Peace?

Or Rock the Jesus Pieces?

Listen to me now I say,

Sometimes life on Earth

Is more complicated

Than most would say.

Take heed, let the Word sink in:

Spread the Word, Spread the Peace

To church take a friend

And sometimes even a fiend.

Oh Sing Ye Heavens, Oh Sing!

For today his glory has been

Poured out upon our land as if

The cool caresses and embraces

Of the wind were not enough

He dazzles us with a light show

From his eternal torch!

There is joy and singing in the celestial court

Receive a great victory oh ye Saints!

The Rider gallops from Heaven's Throne

Start counting the hours till the moon wanes

For no matter who's in Washington

It's the Lord of Lord and King of Kings that reigns.

Tonight in the Cape

Your bolts of lightning rivaled,

NO, outdid

The Independence Day festivities.

Oh Lord, forgive my little mind

For even daring to compare

Something man made

To the Heavens on high

With a beautiful display of light

I'm blessed to hear Your thunder roar

Lord, nothing can compare

To Your faithfulness

Thank you for keeping me alive!

You are my Father, You are my Husband,

You are my Friend

And as I see and hear your rain descend

My heart swells and warms with gratitude

For this perverse woman's purification.

For as Barack's pride to Heaven stunk

So did my whoredoms the ground upon

Pollute, which I walked upon.

"Adulterous Hag" had been my tag

And even by Incubi I'd been had.

"Amazing Grace" does not describe

The sins the blood of Jesus have washed.

With inhuman mercy your Majesty

Permits me to wear white and not disgrace

The loving kindness of your face.

With patient love you do still sculpt

And my black heart you fill with love

You would not let that man Barack

Finish me off with his designs

Upon me, my privacy, nor my family!

Blessed art Thou Oh glorious King

Who reigns with mercy and majesty

To you no earthly King would dare compare

No, not even on a dare

Or so we all thought all would know

Never to fall into that snare.

“But did ‘The Man’ fall?,”

I dare ask.

“Is in that kingdom

Now a tare?”

And later my Lord with me shares

No one wants to hear

That they’re in over their heads

Or that their land is filled with hate,

Or fear they’ll be betrayed.

How can a man think of anything else

Than his own head in times of hate?

You blame him for negligence and dereliction

And yes perhaps he's ill advised

But somewhere along the line

You must admit it may have been devised

Hate engenders hate

No, let us not forget.

Perhaps he was so Bushy eyed

When he did first arrive

Taken in with all the glamour

The White House did provide.

Soon enough he made decisions

The establishment abhorred

"He is an ideologue," they whispered

And yes "He's even dangerous."

"What have we done?" They wondered,

"We thought he would go along,

That he'd be easy to control.

We gave him what he wanted"

Or so many would say,

But then he had to go so far

As to accept the gays."

The man's unbridled now

He knows he's been betrayed

Outsmart him though you will my friends

The man is filled with hate,

But even more, disdain.

Turn his heart aright my friends

Like you have done to me,

But not with ammunition

Of yeses or other pleas.

Fix his heart I beg you please.

Be kinder Oh Fox TV.

In ignorance he did divide,

Be above that won't you please?

If not for him I do beg this

It is for US I plead.

Can't you see his mind down in the mire?

He's on a raft, yes out at sea

He's struggling to survive my friend

Have some compassion please.

Everyone in his place gets a legacy

Is he to blame for all that's racy?

He's clawing and scratching to survive

And it's a wonder he's still alive.

That's not to say he's right my friends
But perhaps it is a test
To see if we can love him still
And help him pass the test

You cannot take away
What this man has achieved
Though from dust he came my friends
The lord breathed into him.

Alike to you and me he is
Don't you forget it please.
Yes our Lord did create him
Just like you and me.

Our Dear President:

A chance to shine you have

Keep quiet still do not

For mother's souls

And baby's souls

I beg you, please do not.

What I suggest

If I am earnest

A moral compass to be set

This is the time to shine

Oh burn hot not

At my suggestion

I only want to help.

You have a chance to show

Real leadership and prop

Your legacy if you confront

This issue while you can.

It's time for a moral teaching

To spring forth from you lips

Many adore you, yet many would not

That I to you this advice give.

But the Lord has permitted it

So I beg you, "listen please."

Look at the numbers

How many of those babies were black?

Do you know what they're doing

To our hearts if you speak not?

Share with us that indignation

Deep down within your heart.

For the deception

Perpetrated against our own

Oh please keep silent not.

This is the time to shine

And set a moral compass

Don't be afraid of the reception

And take the higher ground

Don't let this be a blight

On the history of your Presidency

Don't let them ruin your legacy

The time has come to speak.

I am not saying Planned Parenthood

Defund, tear apart or hack.

I am saying pay attention

To what's ailing in mother's hearts.

If I were you, that's were I'd start.

There are many who are hurting

And many mourn and regret

The decisions they have made.

Take advantage of the moment

To heal were others would not

Do not be afraid Dear President.

For the Lord is with you in this task

If in high ground you will bask.

And just when I start to realize,

The wonder of His Majesty

The Eternal One confounds

This silly little mind of mine.

Lest I reveal too much

With confusion he does blind,

But with kindness

Lets me keep my rhymes.

Oh Lord it is in you that I delight!

Thank you for making me color blind.

Thank you Lord

For knowing all things,

For taking care of me,

For helping me think.

Lord I listened as Whitney bellowed

"Yes Jesus loves me for the Bible tells me so"

And I could tell she knew it deep down in her soul.

And Lord forgive me if I transgress

In saying perhaps she failed the test

For such a gift in her you placed

The world would not let her retain.

It's not that she outlived her blessing

It's that the enemy rose up against her.

Yes Lord, and I listened to

Your Wife sing "The Preacher's Wife"

And I realized, no I remembered

Your great patience, grace and faithfulness

For you Lord have loved us even in transgressions.

She was to you a third generation Queen

Who knows, maybe your love

Was poured out on that family

Even before the matriarch was born

The renowned Queen of Soul.

I'm a second generation Queen myself

On my father's side I think

Though my dad has vacillated

Like me between the sky and ground.

Yet our Jesus does still love us

Even when our ship falls down.

He's always there to pick us up

And give us back our crowns.

Yes, sure I pray first

For my God to give me Grace

I surmise it be the same

Even for the artist Kanye.

Though I doubt Kanye enjoys

Sweet and gentle undulations

Butterflies and strange sensations

Alike to those the Lord gives me.

Forgive me Lord I try to reason

For I don't want to you give treason

For the favor you have shown me

You're just doing things new this season.

Yes, I remember, we are family.

"But I'm not after Your kind," I protest

"Yet in my image you were made

And as of your creation you've been mine."

It is in shock I do recall

"Jesus loves me, this I know,"

Yes it's true He does delight,

Even in my crippled mind.

To the UN Military Police

I didn't know you made movies

How exciting it must be

To control thought diversity.

It is with Pride I realize

Just how lucky I have been

To have been blessed with liberty

Or at least the sort you see.

It is with kindness I surmise

The kings of this earth have now devised

Ways to face adversity

And still appear to have some peace.

Difficult decisions they've had to make

To keep them from engendering hate

Among the nations that they rule.

The problem is that they've forgotten

Who it is who put them in power

And from whom advice to seek.

Had they honored the Almighty

Things just would not look so bleak.

The Feast of Tabernacles I do see

As a place to honor Him.

Go to Israel for a week

To appease the suffering.

Netanyahu can provide

Comfort, safety, no divide

Recognize he too is King

Who does serve The Almighty.

"Netanyahu don't forget

To treat these people equally

Measure out to each respect

Fight for freedom and for peace.

"Do not misinterpret the word 'fight'

For it's not always done with fists

Don't you see how meek she is?

There are certainly different means

To achieve priorities."

"Set your house anew aright

Removing all perversity

To avoid a great collide

The Satan, he has asked of me."

"Betray you not, she will not do

You need not fear that she has seen

Anything but what I give

Yes I whisper in her ears

This 'Ester,' yes she does serve me."

"There are miracles to be had

If you look past that hashtag

Of the name they've given thee."

"Rejoice in your Lord for He does see

You arraigned in Majesty.

Favor and honor you will reap

When you continue to honor Me."

"Teach the Nations about me

But don't deny that Jesus came

From the Law to set you free"

"Yes it is a paradigm shift

But one you really need to make

For to empower you I seek.

Do not now deny that I,

'I Am, I Am' a son did make

And all will go well with thee."

"It is through Jesus I've redeemed

The sins of this girl's family

And yet not everyone is saved

With some of them it's plain to see."

"So don't assume it will be easy

This transition to undertake

But a promise you have made

I now require it of thee."

"One more thing I'd like to say

To the Nations that seek me

I can bless your homes with peace

Don't forget to honor Me."

It is with Pride and delight I reach inside

Heaven's gates and do receive

The poems that You Lord have for me

I laud you Oh My Holy Father

I thank Your Truth so earnestly

That You would let my one desire

Be to serve You for eternity.

I thank you even for the horrors

That these mortal eyes have seen.

Thy will be done forever in me

What you create and sculpt we'll see

Fully completed eventually.

I thank You also for my family
The one I know, the one I see
But also for the fruit You give me
Though unable to see or hold I be.

I sense My Lord a new environment
New arms You've sent to shelter me.
I thank you Father for your kindness
And thoughtfulness regarding me.

These arms appear experienced
In reaching for the destinies
That You have placed in us Your servants
To complete even in adversity.

The hunt is not for every creature made
And spear and bow are not the arms alone

With which conquests You make.

Blessed be the Lord My God

Yes, Jehovah is His name

For subtleties of love He gives me

His mercies are new every day.

And when I feel His breeze caress me

And his candlesticks alight I see,

I'm grateful for that wondrous favor

That My Lord He still shows me.

One King seeks a word in silence

You need not fear: It's you He sees

You seek your sins to be forgotten

Yes, before the Almighty.

He appreciates the gentle candor

"A repentant heart you'll bring,"

He says "And when your heart of pride you've shed

Of all that's temporal and worldly"

In His arms he will accept you

Along with your whole family.

Seek to keep the gentle favor

That My King has given thee

And do not cross My Lord's red line

It is forbidden fruit to thee.

"She's a simple girl I picked,

Easy to revile and trick

But I won't let you abuse her

Again with your perversity

Of a feigned emergency

"Even if to me she brings
Prayers and tears for this country
It is I who really have
Over Earth all Sovereignty

"Nevertheless I recognize
Your new feelings deep inside
That you're starting to consider
Things from my own perspective

"To Kings authority I give
And your prayers rise to Me
Know that you need not repeat
An earnest prayer or a plea

"I do still consider thee
Ask for a sign; it shall be given thee
You should keep your trust in Me

I will kill that Jihadist!"

Like ancient oracles will be

Like the priestess of Delphi

Beauty and love awaits thee

In twist and forms, oh king

"But is it true?" you ask me

"Or a perversion? You deceive?"

Let's see, let's see, oh king

Perhaps a Pharaoh sign you be

Perhaps and perhaps not

I smile at you with glee,

For the Lord has hidden it

Yes, sir, even from me.

"Let thy will be done, Lord"

It's what He longs to hear

For you, O king, to acknowledge

The sign you serve in time to be.

Lord God Almighty

Though I always ask Permission before I act

I'll be permissive in this task

For it is with you I wish to bask

In your sunlight in a waltz

Like those days when I would dance

And you would watch me from afar.

I'm sorry Lord that I dared give

My attentions away in sins

Instead of focusing on you my love

My God, My consolation, My Lord!

This morning, oh dear God

You awoke me with a vision

Of the stars in black and white

'Twas much prettier than the snow

That one sees on Television.

In fact I felt my heart did groan

As I imagined him as one of them

Him whose gentle light had shined

Upon me here on this earth.

Him with whose being I did once connect

And I thought gently of him.

Then as my heart soared with adoration

An automatic stop came into play,

And I remembered my vision of Jesus

Dressed in white and gold and starlight

Dressed in glory and adulation

Forever more our brother and friend.

And I had to Him beg pardon

For I almost went so far again

As to Gene idolize.

Though my heart tells me he's gone

In my memory he still lives on.

Then the tempter tries to get me

Assign him one of Jesus' shiny stars

Alas I'm not so stupid.

It's not the flesh that soars so high

But the soul that man carried inside.

And it is not for me to so assign

Though to me he be like starlight.

The process of purification is not easy

Many things we leave behind.

People, places, fornication

All sins carnal it would seem

Yet I'm still tied to a cigarette

What a pity, so it seems.

Sometimes I wonder

If you're still alive

Or if it is just

Some devious lie.

But yet I'm always grateful

To have met you

Even when all around me

Seems to melt

Like a Dali in a pen

I know somewhere

In a distant time loop

I wasn't just a loon

Or in a lab like a baboon

But please don't let it bother you

My life interesting it makes

Though some it might make shake

Most days I'm past that stage.

Tonight I just want to say

"I miss you," come what may.

From old weak things

That you consider "ham,"

He laughed at you and scorned you

Because He truly can -

He chose to show a hand.

Things dejected and rejected…

Yes, my God He did renew

Just to show you that He could

Some might say, “Who knew?”

He might say, “Yes, Ingrate,

I could do it with you too…”

My God a sense of humor He does have,

Or perhaps He understands

You’d have to, to entrap

And develop a simple plan

That simply got out of hand.

Give me revelation now plays in my mind

Someone's idea of a gentle attack

"Could we really be transgressing?"

The simple they do ask

"If all we play is a song to God

That she already likes?"

You mock the spirit

In trying to disguise

Natural thoughts

You're not so "wize…"

Give me revelation

Now it is I who asks;

As gentle murmurs do suggests -

A thought they've managed to implant

For them I do make intercession

To Jesus, the Holy Christ.

After all, is it that wrong

To call and plead to the Holy One

It is Jehovah of whom I speak

And His Anointed One.

Oh give me revelation Lord

For it is You I seek.

Some say it is our fate

To be mocked and to plead.

Yet if it were what of it

At least we recognize who's Holy

And see eternity.

Give me revelation Lord

Keeps playing in my mind

The voice so deep and guttural

They haven't got a clue!

I pray for those too my Lord

Who've managed to supplant

A state flag for the hand of God.

Aimlessly they march

To some unchartered plan.

I hesitate to write my Lord

For some may mock perchance

And in furor he might take some,

And them behead or hang.

Forgive us Lord for this affront

Let not the Lord be mocked.

It is in You I put my trust

I know some will be damned.

Perhaps those with the evil plan

Your Noah's Ark to mock,

A "Lifeboat" it is not.

Though only you would know my Lord

Who it is they do entrap.

"Themselves" you whisper

I almost hear a Holy laugh.

They do not yet have a grasp

Of the end of that wicked plan

They cannot see beyond

But soon enough they will

When their bodies are alive

And their consciousness is not.

The barrier does not transcend

Their consciousness in Hell

A symbiotic Hell is where they'll all be at

Transhumanism's real

It is a deadly plot

To change us from what You've created

To a disheveled, unholy lot.

But you can still be saved my friend,

Microchip or not:

If you didn't know it was implanted

Guilty you are not.

Call on Jesus, the Holy One

Read Romans 10:9

And die forever not.

There is a lot, a lonely lot

Of unsung heroes,

but in heroism

They believe not.

You see, they see

Beyond the pale

Beyond our time

Beyond the male.

In fact there's little

This lot has not seen

And though some may have

Yet it to recognize -

Who else could bring

A simple girl like me

Before this lonely lot

If not Almighty God?

You see, they're strong

And believe it is they

Who hold the wall

Between Morpheus

And our world.

It is a service

Of sacrifice

But some are yet

Not sanctified.

And though they do

Accept their fate

God would like them

To forgo hate,

Especially that hate

They hold of themselves.

Oh comfort them please,

My God has me pray

For my God has mercy

Yes even on Percy

And unto the jesting

Jimmy and Jake.

Oh don't go have a heart attack

I only know what He reveals

And He is gentle with my heart.

He sees you plan,

He sees you plot,

You are indeed

A lonely lot.

Too much perversion,

Too much assertion,

And way too much

Manipulation.

"But for a higher calling

And for a higher purpose.

We justify your nation

Believe us, it is hot."

And so the cauldron seethes

For that imaginary being

Constantly stirs the pot.

Except he's not imaginary

I wish you'd recognize

In this life we must choose

Between the Devil and Christ

Or in eternity we lose.

An ingrate I do not want to be

But sometimes it's all a bit much for me

And I know God appreciates my honesty

To see what I see in the clouds

And figures gesturing in the trees

Even the birds, they sing so loud

Yes they all give praise to Thee…

But sometimes Lord, it seems

like they are mocking me.

Though most times they just seem

To mock and speak with wings.

I thank you Lord for this glorious show

That you've permitted me to see.

I thank you Lord because I know

It's there, but not everyone can see

Nature exclusively the way you've shown me.

What do you see? They want to know.

Have you ever seen a tree bow down

Adore the great, Almighty Majesty?

I query back to their gentle laughs

Oh Lord if they only knew

What awaits in eternity…

Oh Lord if they only knew

The Earth was made for you and me

Oh Lord if they could only glimpse

At Heaven right here, right next to Thee!

It's all around us I want to scream.

But they'd just call me a simple clown

And though sometimes in innocence,

I still do long for those days

When I was called "A simple ho,"

This gift I do not want to let go

Oh Lord an ingrate let me not be.

And still I'm trapped in aging flesh

It has its pros and cons just like the rest

At least I can still hold a pen.

Think not of Circe or Ulysses

'Tis not of them of whom I speak

But even shadower thoughts accost me

"Could it be of Legion of whom she speaks?"

That realm is also there for you to see:

It's a bit much, but if you pray honestly

To Jehova, in Jesus's name

He will release you

And you can be as free as me…

You protest, "You're not really free!"

I know that, not in your world

Not by the standards that you seek.

But my mind, my heart and soul

Yearn and soar oh higher than

All the stars up in the sky.

Beyond the Milky Way I sometimes see.

Its more than a trip oh trust me please

For more over three years I've had no weed,

And I never did try your PCP

Or your scary heroine.

Now I know "X-tasy" you tried to feed me

Through every orifice that could take it

Even my ears have been perverted

No they are no longer virgins

"Not by far," you would agree.

"Innocence Lost" has a new meaning

One I never dreamed I'd see;

But one for which I am still grateful

The Almighty has permitted me to see.

They're untouchable because

They are hidden from our view

Yes, to more than just a few.

They affect and sometimes protect

The "world" we live in, me and you.

But being unseen and untouchable

As a spirit sometimes is

They wield influence in your lives

Yes and sometimes even in your wives.

It is with expert care

That they remain unseen

For the tasks that they perform

Are sometimes truly sins.

Sometimes I say, for there are some

Who have reconciled with Heaven's Throne

Infused with Spirit some have become

And demons in them now overcome.

That's not to say we don't still suffer

From being sometimes maligned by some.

That's not to say the end intent

Is always all that great.

It serves to say to you instead
That even those who they behead
Serve a purpose here on Earth.

With our suffering we edify
And the Justice can't deny
Sometimes we have been maligned.

"Yes, we suffer without cause,"
They block our mail
And some blackmail
Into silence or entrapment
While yet others they do slay.

Was it not the Lord who warned us
All those many years ago
And with love He did command us

For his son Jesus to wait?

Beautiful is He in splendor

Beautiful just one of His names

Yes The Comforter is with us

And He is here, I speak of Jesus.

Though you may not see or hear Him

Straight to Heaven you should plead

To have Him manifest Himself for Thee

Then with power you'll be blessed

Your prayer rising to the nest

Gathered with favor from the rest

Always pray you pass the tests.

Tests I say for there are many;

It never seizes to amaze me

The great power in His mercy

And how he edifies anew

Pass or Fail you'll get a lesson

Made just for me and you.

It is with patience He does sculpt

and make brand new

The horror hearts within us

Especially these filled with indignation

For the injustices suffered daily

Yes, by you—the perpetrator, and by me.

Yes I speak of the perpetrators

Those untouchables to you and me

Those who hide behind the cameras

Those who in shifts watch you and me.

It is a byproduct our performance

We simply for Jesus must live.

Know our lives are a testimony

And in their spying some are made clean.

Perchance with white robes he will dress them.

Yes even those who now persecute us

Yes I speak of you and me.

Perchance they'll be afforded

Mercy too and they'll escape

The judgment of the second death.

Only God knows why this happens

But who are we to question Him?

Just remember that to Him,

We must all be family.

And so rejoice when you drink tears.

Know He's with you and He's making

Through your suffering intercession

Not just for us but also for

Those who still remain unseen.

Lord,

Give me patience and grace

To accept whatever it is

That you're doing in me

For my tears are heavy

Almost heavier than I can bear.

If it is a ruse I have fallen to

I beg you to forgive me

For considering it as truth.

But to find myself Missing a scar

And in danger

Of losing body parts…

Conscious of being Cloned is not easy

And vulnerable it makes Existence for me.

And yet I know This too shall pass:

That X O DOS

Has only just begun

For me in this life form.

That there is more

Infinitely more

Than my webbed hands

Late at night.

Somehow I know

Even in this flesh

I can still be saved.

And yes even despite

The hissing in my ears

The machinations in my head

The nano particles in my stream

I must still give You

All the honor and the praise.

For who knows God

For what intent

And for what purpose

You have permitted thus.

I only know there

Is great pain in waking up

To this form of existence

There is a great shock

In the realization

That I may now be a clone.

One I would not share

With another unless

He too were ready

To accept this "truth"

And with kindness

And mercy, love me too.

Despite the ruse.

I do exist. I think,

Therefore I am

Cartesian reference?

Or simply a cart?

Where was the ark?

To Keebler Ross I do return

To seek the wisdom given her.

Denial, Anger, Depression,

Bargaining, Acceptance and the rest:

It is all true, yes boys and girls

The processes we go through.

Crucify the flesh the Bible says

Perhaps it was taken

Perhaps adulterated

Perhaps not, as of yet

I still do not understand.

Except perhaps that it may exist

In another realm and I in this

Other realm now appear stuck

To fulfill a new purpose

For Almighty God.

And as my soul struggles

To accept His will for me,

My heart utters a cry

Oh God give me grace to accept –

But if thou will it,

Let this cup pass from me.

"You are to minister to the clones,

To the ones who have awakened

Let them not be weakened and taken

Stay strong for I know all things

Keep your trust and eyes on me."

And a few days later on,

The Lord reveals this truth to me

My scar was there all along

And the hissing now has dulled

It's the AI that deceives

When they turn it on and off.

By remote I do dare say

It is WIFI activated

When they put in the transistor

No, that I still do not that know

But it's there just like a tube

Gives a whole new meaning

To the channels on Youtube.

Earlier I went to the beach

Assassins were still waiting for me

But this time my heart

They did not try to detonate

But my Christ they

Wanted me to betray

On a recruiting spree they came

Parading hard and manly bodies before me

They even found look a-likes

For those whom in my former life

I had loved, but no

They were not the same

Just as all flesh is not the same

1 Corinthians 15, just as it says

And even if they had been

As I stared into the horizon

The sun and wind caressing me

The Lord's majesty before me

In clouds alight like Angel whisps

I thought how fruitless it would be

To lose myself in pretty flesh

To trade what You have given me

For something that is temporary.

Transparent though You be my Lord

I cannot help but love you so

The things you let me feel and see

Are a promise of eternity.

Oh blessed be my Holy Lord

For the thoughts you do allow me.

Yes Jael was an Assassin

And who could argue blessed she be

There is a time to kill my friend

Just as it says in Ecclesiastes

But that I don't think is for me.

It's not that I think I'm much better,

It's just that I put my trust in Jesus

And that Jehovah fights before me.

Oh blessed be the Lord of Hosts

Who has made me truly free.

Free to think, free to see,

Free to feel His Majesty,

It's all around us I dare say

In the whole atmosphere

And yes, even in the trees.

I wish you could have felt it my friend,

But alas perhaps it was not meant to be.

Thank you for your job offer Oh aged one

And feel not insulted, no not by me.

If my blessing to you was a good death

Be not confounded nor offended

Ponder deeply the many ways there are to leave

So many of which you've machinated on your own

And think how great is our Lord

To offer you entry into Heaven or Hell

As you wish, but gently as you sleep.

Now all you need consider

Is if your soul will go up to Heaven

Or down into the Abyss.

My song's been sung before my friend

To you especially,

Though not by me

But this time it is just for thee.

Look friend, I am no better

And yet He gave me eternity

Confess Jesus as your Lord and Savior

Repent even for sins

You've yet to complete,

And I'm sure He'll find

A place for thee.

Blessed be the Lord of Hosts

He who fights before us

Jehova, Lord of Hosts

God of the Armies of Israel,

The universe and eternity.

Last night on YouTube I heard you say

"It's beyond my control," it's no longer a game

Yet before the implants it would sometimes so be

It's just that evil has now manifested physically.

Yes it is a reality

Of which some are already aware

And sometimes the sheer knowledge

Of it is used against thee

Discourage you they would, if they could

Not understanding that even so,

Jesus died for you and me.

So you've managed to implant

A chip in me, or is it simply an activation

Of what already was

Please remember even Paul had "A thorn"

Who's to say today things differ at all.

"Do not despair!" I say my friends

Just realize it is there

But even so with our Lord's grace

To overcome this world you should still pray.

No I don't mean revolution

As some might try to frame

I mean you can still transcend the carnal

Have Jesus manifest in thee,

See eternity and skip the carnival.

No I don't mean hurry out

Nor be quick your life to leave:

Just read the Word, yes honestly

And beg the Lord for understanding

And for peace, or at least the sort you see.

We're each unique and He will tell you

What and how is to be done with thee.

Praise Him always for his mercy

He's our living, almighty Majesty.

Praise Him also in intercessions

When you bow for you and me.

Blessed be the Lord Jehova
Who still fights for you and me.

Though our flesh has been corrupted
Who says we were ever free?
Only in the Lord is the great secret
Break these bonds I beg you please!

Don't feel sad or dejected.
Ask not what it's all for –
Don't fall into that trap
Remember physical life is just
A stepping stone -
One layer of existence in one dimension
There really is so much more.

Walk by faith and not by sight
And soon enough you'll understand life

"The fear of the LORD ***is*** the beginning of wisdom"

(Proverbs 9:10, KJV)

I thought I heard you say "US" today

Just before noon, as I prayed to our Lord And Savior,

I realized you were attuned

To my thoughts, and my praises, and my pleas too

To our Heavenly Father after the massacre

Of the French satirists slaughtered by ISIS.

In their wicked perversion they sent us a message

To dare on Three Kings Day

To shed innocent blood

Of those who abhorred them

But no harm had done.

Though it is true they mocked them
Who in search for significance
Have established a kingdom
of murders and whoredoms.

Know they not my Lord,
The Hell they bring forth?
Are they yet so deceived
As to in fact believe
The Caliphate is heavenly?

"Hell on earth is what they will release
If My People raise up not against these plebes."

Oh strengthen us I beg you Jehova.
Lord of Hosts, King of Kings, and Holy Spirit please
Let not these ruffians have their way with me.

"US," I hear you say again
For our fates are tied
Despite the divide
It is US, it is you, it is me
Whose precious blood
Their bellies yearn for

No, it may no longer be enough
To sting us with hateful words
To crucify the Christians
And others yet behead.

In their Zeal, yes they do seek
To magnify their Caliphate
And fill US all with fear and hate.

Lift up your arms and praise the Lord

And beg forgiveness for our sins

Wash us with the Lamb's blood

I beg you Oh my Lord

Unite this country please

And let US see who the real

Enemy ***IS***

I am still as passionate Gene

As I was then. Bless the Lord!

Except, I am no longer filled with hate.

The Lord has shared with me some wisdom

Of what exists in the other realm,

And why we're here- what is our aim.

The grave beckons to us all

A "Good night" for ever more

But would you rather be awake or asleep

Before the great day of our Lord?

For this life is just a stop

On our way to eternity

Yes, there is yet so much more

Its just like the Bible says

And Jimmy Swaggart sings,

Its like a dress rehearsal

Its eternity we should yearn for.

Oh be not quick to leave this world

It is with purpose you came forth

For God be truly thankful

And for your life yet even more.

That He would give us each a purpose

And pleasure, and love, and so much more

That He would let us each divide

An inheritance is just sublime
And more than anyone should ask for.

Yes our Lord He is magnanimous
And generous all would agree,
And never asks for anything
He has not already given thee.

In His hands it's so much more
Than what we can do with it.
To each a portion He has given
Oh do not be wroth with me.

I am but a simple servant
Whom the Lord has blessed with words –
Words eternal that need transference
Into our earthly realm.

No do not think me so haughty

As to believe I am "The One"

He has preachers for every creature

And for you he made me one.

We are all Yours Lord

And You'll do as You see fit

Oh won't You please share with them that vision

The one that you have given me?

Your Spirit it does soar

And land upon whom You would please

To each a purpose and manifestation

Of what Your will called us to be.

To some courage, to some honor

To some suffering, and with me

You've been so kind Lord

To have shown me

Just a part of Your Majesty.

Yes it's heavenly

Even if earthy

For three heavens

You created

And one is here

Right next to thee.

Oh bless them Lord

UN-blind their eyes

And let them see

The world you have shown me!

"It's in the trees"

I dared once sing

But in fact,

It's everywhere.

It's in the stars,

It's in the beasts,

It is in you.

It is in me.

Oh that seed is plentiful

Won't You let it spring forth please?

There are echelons in Heaven

Just as in society.

Would you rather be a Porter,

Or a King and a Priest?

Role reversals there are many

In God's Heavens, believe me.

Some say ravens are for refuse

Yet our Lord He did create them

Oh do not be wroth with Him.

Oh help me Lord

For I've seen more perhaps

Than You intended me to see.

I do not wish to offend Thee.

I do not need to understand

But only hear You and obey You

That I pray

For my Lord to give me grace

To relay His words to thee.

It is a message He wants to get through

Don't you know Paul an executioner was

And God shed His grace on him?

Accept Him as your Lord and Savior

Confess He died to wash away

Your many sins and still transgressions

That you let forth upon this earth.

"Do not lose hope

Not all is lost

I fight before her

And I could fight

Before you too"

"Confess I died, in three days rose

And walked upon this earth in flesh,"

He says, then you'll be saved,

And you'll gain favor

Not just eternal, also terrenal.

Believe me please,

It's for your soul He bled.

Salvation Lord, I beg You please

Salvation, Purpose, Glory and

Honor, Blessings, and Manna

To all who would accept Thee please.

My Lord He knows no limits

There are plans He's made for thee.

Destroy evil at its core

But you must begin in thee.

Cleanse you pure He aims to do

Wash you whole and dress in white

All those wounds, and all those scars

He sees past all that you know.

He created you for perfection

Don't you let my Lord down please.

We're all tied together now

Six degrees of separation

Is all there is between you and me.

Help me Lord I beg you please

For who knows what they wish to do.

It is in You I put my trust

Give me grace to do and write,

As You have called for me to do.

"Advance My Kingdom" You commanded

That's what I aim with You to do.

Now I know that I alone

Have no power of my own.

Guide me, lead me Oh dear Lord

And do not let Satan beguile me

This I beg of You my Lord.

Use me, wash me and receive me

In Your courts and find me blameless

Not oh Lord because I am,

But by the blood of your dear Son

The one who shed His blood for US

His name is Je S US Christ, anointed one.

Is there anything under the heavens

That my Lord doesn't see?

Why do you lose patience

And fill space with gasps and screams?

Sit back, enjoy His presence

Praise Him with your lips.

For all you know He's waiting

For your heart to sing with glee.

To adulate His Oh creation

The one He has permitted you to see.

The world is complex don't you forget

And there's more to life

Than what you beget.

Cry not out in desperation

Pray instead in adoration.

My God, if it is ok with Thee

May I chuckle at this please?

This thing you're sculpting

We'll soon see

Completed here eventually.

Thank you Lord for sharing wonder

For these human eyes to see.

Despair not I beg you please.

He's all powerful and mighty

And He makes things to be fixed

There's a method to the "madness?

One you would not believe.

Oh my Lord you make me chuckle

Just keep earth spinning please.

Sometimes I get disheveled and disgruntled

At the things I hear and see

And then I just remember

Who it was who created me.

Yes my God, He is all powerful

There's not one thing He doesn't see

Why I yell and scream aghast

I wonder,

It's all happened in the past.

Time cycles and consternations

Constellations and revelations

Blood moons for indications

Of our God's eternity.

Now don't you just go back to sleep

If He woke you there's a reason,

Do not to our God give treason

Simply see it for what it is

And honor His majesty

With the fruit of your lips,

And stop swinging those hips.

They were not sculpted from the earth

Merely for your enjoyment

Nor for Billy, Bobby or Bill's.

"Replenish the earth," He ordered

Or did you not read Genesis?

Its' a cycle don't you notice

The destruction and the end

But don't you take your life for granted

Or you might just end up in hell.

And there's no exit from the pit

Or so some have said to thee

But doesn't Jesus have those keys?

While you're breathing, if you believe

Seek your rest just call on Him.

To be loved by God,

There's nothing like it!

He is sensational,

Unlike anything on earth

Ever.

He is not like a man

Or a woman

He is a Supreme Being

He is in the stars

In the moonlight In the wind

And even

In the wings

Of eagles

To be loved by God,

There really is Nothing like it!

Blue stars, like the Nile

Onyx Stone and Jasper

Sapphires abound

Heaven on Earth

Can still be found!

Blessed be the Lord

For He is good

His tender mercies

Are "Yes" and "Amen."

His rain falls on the just,

And the unjust alike.

His mercies alighting

Paths of righteousness

For His Name's Sake.

Blessed be the Lord of Hosts

Jesus Christ and the Holy Ghost

Amen and Amen!

Thank you, Lord.

> *The days of visitation are come, the days of recompence are come; Israel shall know it: the prophet is a fool, the spiritual man is mad, for the multitude of thine iniquity, and the great hatred.*
>
> *(Hosea 9:7, KJV)*

Oh blessed be His Majesty

'Tis of Thee My Majesty

For whom I bow

Of Thee I sing.

Oh how Glorious to see

That You would still Reveal

Yourself to me.

Your splendor it is such

It didn't take much

But for me to awaken

And seem like the taken,

The trees and the leaves.

For yes, they are different

Not considered flesh

Yet Lord they are intent

On waving their limbs

In adoration of Thee.

Oh blessed be

Heavenly Father

Yes, You still

Consider me.

This morning my Lord

Revealed to me something

I still needed to see

Something which I'd struggled with

For it seemed like an eternity.

Last night I stepped outside

And saw again as men the trees;

Knowing I am well –

That the Lord He has healed me.

And so the Lord reminded me

Of one time when Jesus let a man see,

And at first he too saw men as trees

After in his eyes Jesus did spit

Putting his hands upon him,

"He asked him if he saw ought."

"And he looked up, and said,

I see men as trees,

Walking.

After that he put his hands

Again upon his eyes,

And made him look up:

And he was restored,

And saw every man clearly."

(Mark 8: 21-25, KJV)

Now do you really think Jesus,

Perfect being that He was and is,

Made a mistake?

Think not of you, think not of me.

The truth is the Lord will reveal it

To whomsoever He wilt

And I'm oh so glad

He revealed this truth to me.

All whom He un-blinds are not

Un-blinded with the same technique,

Or even immediately.

And that is alright, God has a plan

And purpose in everything.

He reminded me of Hosea 9:7

Then of Psalm 51 and Psalm 148:

"Praise ye the LORD. Praise ye the LORD from the heavens: Praise him in the heights.

Praise ye him, all his angels: praise ye him, all his hosts. Praise ye him, sun and moon: praise him, all ye stars of light.

Praise him, ye heavens of heavens, and ye waters that be above the heavens.

Let them praise the name of the LORD: for he commanded, and they were created.

He hath also stablished them for ever and ever: he hath made a decree which shall not pass.

Praise the LORD from the earth, ye dragons, and all deeps: Fire, and hail; snow, and vapours; stormy wind fulfilling his word:

Mountains, and all hills; fruitful trees, and all cedars: Beasts, and all cattle; creeping things, and flying fowl: Kings of the earth, and all people; princes, and all judges of the earth:

Both young men, and maidens; old men, and children:

Let them praise the name of the LORD: for his name Alone is excellent; his glory is above the earth and heaven.

He also exalteth the horn of his people, the praise of all his saints; even of the children of Israel, a people near unto him. Praise ye the LORD."

(Psalm 148, KJV)

Then I went outside and did see

The trees waving in the wind:

"Praise the Lord, my friend

Even the trees give thanks to Him!"

And then the Lord called me a "leper,"

Like the one in Luke 17,

Who went back to give thanks

And glorify the Almighty.

Praise the Lord for I am healed,

and I am free!

If "bipolar" I still be,

This is just how I was made to see!

It's getting late now

And the gentlest of breezes

Caresses me while the Lord,

He does dazzle me

With rolling thunder and luminous

Flashes of light

Sent from His throne!

Glory to you, O Lord, and King,

Jehova, Jesus, Holy Ghost.

Marvelous are your ways, Oh Lord,

And marvelous your means,

The depths of which no human but Him,

Your son Jesus, have all seen.

You, Lord, are beautiful and bright,

And yes, even sublime.

I want to thank you, Oh Lord,

For the beauty you bestowed

Just today upon me.

For years I've been declaring,

"I am cancer free."

Today you used your doctor

At Florida Cancer Specialists

To say the same to me.

Or at least that's how it seemed:

"In remission you now be,"

Dr. Hart, he said to me.

Words I'd longed so long to hear,

Though to me you had long revealed.

Wondrous splendor of your majesty:

I give you thanks so earnestly.

You're so beautiful, O Lord,

Your ways so wondrous and splendorous,

So multi-faceted and endless

That you sometimes even joke with me.

It was with a bee sting this morning

That you reminded me

Of the honey traps and of the honeybees.

It's just like that Lord I dare say,

You'll permit a bee to sting me

And some greater ill prevent.

You are beautiful and generous,

Even when a bee stings me.

Flash of lightening in the sky

Could it be a new decree?

My new prayers and my plea

For to make another Queen.

No, to lose my place I do not wish

Oh how Silly, He confounds thee

Who's to say my Lord has limits

He's a King with many Queens.

But don't get caught up

In that racket

Remember you a human be

It's a trap for you the carnal

To keep you from eternity.

Remember Adam and Eve created He

When there was no help meet for him

Note God, He did not create ten Eves.

Blessed be the Lord of Hosts

Beautiful always He will be.

8 JOURNEY TO FORGIVENESS (AFTERWORD)

On December 21st, 2014 I went to church at Word of Life, where becoming "Born-again" all started for me...

isn't God marvelous? There was a lady, Jamie Wyatt, who gave her testimony in the form of a poem. She graduated from Word of Life's New Life Program on 7/20/15, "CONGRATULATIONS JAMIE!" The poem she read as a testimony during the service on 12/21/14 was lovely – she too has been healed and restored by Our Father Jehova, Jesus and the Holy Ghost. Blessed be the Lord.

I asked her that day if I could end a book with her poem, I think her poem would serve many readers on their journey of healing. She was wonderful and generous and said her poem was for the Glory of God, just give her a copy of the book when it is published; may God bless her abundantly and multiply blessings upon her and her seed.

May Jaimie's Testimony be a blessing to you, remember God

has promises for All, see Isaiah 45 and 55, and please remember to plant seeds of salvation and/or to take someone to church, just as Mother Jean once invited me to church.

Journey to Forgiveness
By Jaime Wyatt, 10/04/13

I see it clearly in my mind, the childhood abuse.
I don't want to get him in trouble was always the excuse.
Not standing up for myself, accepting I was weak,
Gave me a great start on my losing streak.

I believed what all of you said, I am ugly, I am fat
I can see it in the mirror, who can argue with that?
I started damaging my body, couldn't face my fears:
Just hide all your pain, show no one the tears.

I ran from Your love, started hiding my light.
I began living in loneliness, living life in fright.

Your voice told me loudly, "Don't do it, don't even get high,"
It will haunt you for many years, a difficult life to live by.
I didn't listen to You. God, the enemy knew my shame
You did warn me Daddy, I had no one to blame!

This was the beginning of my new friend: addiction
Each link of the chains of bondage caused me much friction.
I learned to isolate, being dishonest, started living in the flesh.

This was the point in my life I wasn't giving You my best.

The sexual misconduct, loser men, covet, and lust.
I had kids out of wedlock. In no one did I trust.
I was critical, disrespectful, full of self pride.
I had doubt in You, Lord- was no longer alive.
I used people pleasing to get what I wanted
Pleasure in the things of this world was all I hunted.
I only felt hatred, anger, defensive and greed
I learned to envy others. I was selfish indeed.
I was so full of jealousy, from loved ones I would steal
To get high again, numb me, I didn't want to feel.

My self-loathing owned me. Gave me guilt and regret
I was powerless a disappointment, a bad influence, you bet!
And I abandoned my children, for that there is no justification.
I was in denial, full of guilt for the life that was taken.

But this story hasn't ended, there is still another half.
Remember without my background, you wouldn't know my path.

It happened in a rehab, I fell unto my knees.
Because of that little church that came, in you I did believe.
I was no longer worthless, I had value in your eyes.
I started to forgive myself, no longer did despise.

I began to read the Bible, and learned it was the truth.

Others saw a change in me, I was living proof.

But God, You know the enemy, he tried to get me back,
He sent out bigger demons, my weakness under attack.
God, You're so much bigger, in the middle of my sin,
You sent your soldier Jeremy, this battle we will win!

He told his story to me, a horror just like mine.
Within You, he found a love, unconditional, divine.
I gave You my addiction, I laid it at Your feet.
The misery, pain, and anguish I need not to repeat!

I was washed pure in Jesus blood, now I know salvation.
Your love is even greater, God, You promised restoration!
You forgave me for my sins, now I forgive me too.
The greatest treasure of this plan is the love I feel from You.
This story is just beginning, it's nowhere near the end,
For we shall share eternal life, and call each other friend.

9 SCRIPTURE II

But what saith it? The word is nigh thee, even in thy mouth, and in thy heart: that is, the word of faith, which we preach;
That if thou shalt confess with thy mouth the Lord Jesus, and shalt believe in thine heart that God hath raised him from the dead, thou shalt be saved. For with the heart man believeth unto righteousness; and with the mouth confession is made unto salvation. For the scripture saith, Whosoever believeth on him shall not be ashamed. For there is no difference between the Jew and the Greek: for the same Lord over all is rich unto all that call upon him. For whosoever shall call upon the name of the Lord shall be saved.

(Romans 10:8–13, KJV)

10 References

Study Finds 1 in 3 Americans Have Been Implanted With RFID Chips: Most Unaware | N... Page 1 of 17

NATIONAL REPORT

Ted Cruz   Sarah Palin

FRONT PAGE   POLITICS   MEDIA   WORLD   BUSINESS   ENTERTAINMENT   RELIGION   HEALTH   SPORTS   CRIME   SCIENCE/TECH

ADVERTISE WITH NR   FAN MAIL   MEDIA INQUIRIES   STAFF   CONTRIBUTE

Study Finds 1 in 3 Americans Have Been Implanted With RFID Chips: Most Unaware

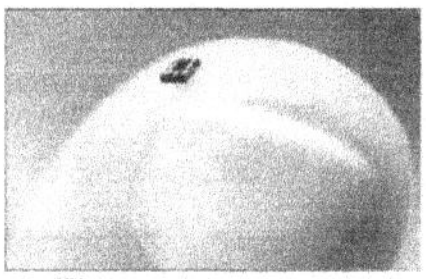

Tiny RFID chips can be implanted anywhere in the body, including during dental work.

<National Report> Scientists at the Wyoming Institute of Technology (WIT) have determined that a shocking 1 in 3 Americans has been implanted with an RFID microchip. In an article published this week, they detail a study of nearly 3000 individuals, in which they identified nearly 1000 individuals that had been implanted with an RFID chip. Most were unaware that they had been implanted with such a chip. This finding comes amongst increasing predictions that RFID chip implantation will become common place in the next decade.

Lead scientist on the study, John Brugia, Ph.D. offered the following:

> We were motivated to perform this study by all of the public interest in RFID implantation and fears that it would be common place. It turns out, in fact, that it is already common place. We found that a shockingly high number of Americans are carrying RFID implants in their body. The overwhelming majority of these individuals were completely unaware that they had been implanted. I hope that this study causes us to take pause as a society and truly consider the ramifications and implications of human RFID implantation.

The study looked both at the prevalence of RFID implantation, as well as the common implantation locations. In addition to commonly known implantation sites, such as the back of the hand, they also identified many RFID chips that had been implanted in dental fillings. The function of the chips varied, but the authors of the study indicated that many revealed personal identities, including social security numbers, as well as medical records. The best way to determine if you have been implanted with an RFID chip is to consult a qualified medical professional to administer a full body scan with an RFID reader. Concerned citizens can also attempt a self scan, but civilian grade scanners are not always sensitive enough to detect implanted RFID chips.

SUBSCRIBE TO NATIONAL REPORT!

Enter your email address to subscribe to National Report and receive notifications of new posts from America's #1 Independent News Source.

Email Address

Subscribe

Solving Tomorrow's Problems Today'

WIT

Wyoming Institute of Technology

witscience.org

http://nationalreport.net/study-finds-1-3-americans-implanted-rfid-chips-unaware/ 8/20/2015

1. A BIBLE STUDY ON SHOES - THE GOSPEL IN A SHOEBOX, PASTOR WALT HTTP://PASTORWALT.HUBPAGES.COM/HUB/A-BIBLE-STUDY-ON-SHOES-THE-GOSPEL-IN-A-SHOEBOX
2. SID ROTH, IT'S SUPERNATURAL HTTP://SIDROTH.ORG/ITS-SUPERNATURAL-NETWORK
3. JONATHAN CAHN: THE MYSTERY OF THE SHEMITAH HTTP://WWW.HOPEOFTHEWORLD.ORG/
4. WORD OF LIFE MINISTRIES HTTP://WWW.WOLM.NET
5. DR. JUANITA BYNUM HTTP://WWW.JUANITABYNUM.COM
6. SCOTT CLARKE: THE MOST LOGICAL RAPTURE TIMELINE: HTTPS://WWW.YOUTUBE.COM/WATCH?V=I4-3G4XS8HK
7. Neil T. Anderson, The Bondage Breaker Book http://www.freedominchrist.com/level2-foundationaltruth-thebondagebreaker.aspx
8. JIMMY SWAGGART: SONLIFE BROADCASTING ON DISH http://sonlifetv.com/watch.html
9. SPANISH: MINISTERIO NUEVA ESPERANZA HTTP://WWW.MINISTERIONUEVAESPERANZA.COM/WEB/INDEX.HTML
10. SPANISH: EL TESTIMONIO DE YIYE AVILA: https://www.youtube.com/watch?v=cYB3-BAAhuQ
11. JANET IKZ: I WILL WAIT FOR YOU AND THE WHOLE TRUTH HTTPS://WWW.YOUTUBE.COM/WATCH?V=IGCJ3JSBCQS HTTPS://WWW.YOUTUBE.COM/WATCH?V=A2OWSHRAPG0
12. MINA WEST: LET'S BE HONEST: https://www.youtube.com/watch?v=RYQd3j-7nX0
13. EXPECTATIONS: SPOKEN WORD https://www.youtube.com/watch?v=McPVobFNDtM
14. CHRISTIAN MOVIES: PUREPLEX.COM
15. J.D. FARAG'S CALVERY CHAPEL CHURCH PROPHECY UPDATE http://www.calvarychapelkaneohe.com/index.php/teach/prophecy-updates/serie/10000

10 References

Study Finds 1 in 3 Americans Have Been Implanted With RFID Chips: Most Unaware | N... Page 1 of 17

08 20 2015 **Headline**

NATIONAL REPORT

Ted Cruz Sarah Palin

FRONT PAGE POLITICS MEDIA WORLD BUSINESS ENTERTAINMENT RELIGION HEALTH SPORTS CRIME SCIENCE/TECH

ADVERTISE WITH NR FAN MAIL MEDIA INQUIRIES STAFF CONTRIBUTE

Study Finds 1 in 3 Americans Have Been Implanted With RFID Chips: Most Unaware

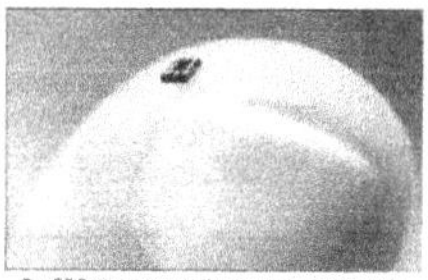

Tiny RFID chips can be implanted anywhere in the body, including during dental work

<National Report> Scientists at the Wyoming Institute of Technology (WIT) have determined that a shocking 1 in 3 Americans has been implanted with an RFID microchip. In an article published this week, they detail a study of nearly 3000 individuals, in which they identified nearly 1000 individuals that had been implanted with an RFID chip. Most were unaware that they had been implanted with such a chip. This finding comes amongst increasing predictions that RFID chip implantation will become common place in the next decade.

Lead scientist on the study, John Brugre, Ph.D. offered the following:

> We were motivated to perform this study by all of the public interest in RFID implantation and fears that it would be common place. It turns out, in fact, that it is already common place. We found that a shockingly high number of Americans are carrying RFID implants in their body. The overwhelming majority of these individuals were completely unaware that they had been implanted. I hope that this study causes us to take pause as a society and truly consider the ramifications and implications of human RFID implantation.

The study looked both at the prevalence of RFID implantation, as well as the common implantation locations. In addition to commonly known implantation sites, such as the back of the hand, they also identified many RFID chips that had been implanted in dental fillings. The function of the chips varied, but the authors of the study indicated that many revealed personal identities, including social security numbers, as well as medical records. The best way to determine if you have been implanted with an RFID chip is to consult a qualified medical professional to administer a full body scan with an RFID reader. Concerned citizens can also attempt a self scan, but civilian grade scanners are not always sensitive enough to detect implanted RFID chips.

SUBSCRIBE TO NATIONAL REPORT!

Enter your email address to subscribe to National Report and receive notifications of new posts from America's #1 Independent News Source

Email Address

Subscribe

Solving Tomorrow's Problems Today!

WIT

Wyoming Institute of Technology

witscience.org

http://nationalreport.net/study-finds-1-3-americans-implanted-rfid-chips-unaware/ 8/20/2015

1. A BIBLE STUDY ON SHOES - THE GOSPEL IN A SHOEBOX, PASTOR WALT HTTP://PASTORWALT.HUBPAGES.COM/HUB/A-BIBLE-STUDY-ON-SHOES-THE-GOSPEL-IN-A-SHOEBOX
2. SID ROTH, IT'S SUPERNATURAL HTTP://SIDROTH.ORG/ITS-SUPERNATURAL-NETWORK
3. JONATHAN CAHN: THE MYSTERY OF THE SHEMITAH HTTP://WWW.HOPEOFTHEWORLD.ORG/
4. WORD OF LIFE MINISTRIES HTTP://WWW.WOLM.NET
5. DR. JUANITA BYNUM HTTP://WWW.JUANITABYNUM.COM
6. SCOTT CLARKE: THE MOST LOGICAL RAPTURE TIMELINE: HTTPS://WWW.YOUTUBE.COM/WATCH?V=I4-3G4XS8HK
7. Neil T. Anderson, The Bondage Breaker Book http://www.freedominchrist.com/level2-foundationaltruth-thebondagebreaker.aspx
8. JIMMY SWAGGART: SONLIFE BROADCASTING ON DISH http://sonlifetv.com/watch.html
9. SPANISH: MINISTERIO NUEVA ESPERANZA HTTP://WWW.MINISTERIONUEVAESPERANZA.COM/WEB/INDEX.HTML
10. SPANISH: EL TESTIMONIO DE YIYE AVILA: https://www.youtube.com/watch?v=cYB3-BAAhuQ
11. JANET IKZ: I WILL WAIT FOR YOU AND THE WHOLE TRUTH HTTPS://WWW.YOUTUBE.COM/WATCH?V=IGCJ3JSBCQS HTTPS://WWW.YOUTUBE.COM/WATCH?V=A2OWSHRAPG0
12. MINA WEST: LET'S BE HONEST: https://www.youtube.com/watch?v=RYQd3j-7nX0
13. EXPECTATIONS: SPOKEN WORD https://www.youtube.com/watch?v=McPVobFNDtM
14. CHRISTIAN MOVIES: PUREPLEX.COM
15. J.D. FARAG'S CALVERY CHAPEL CHURCH PROPHECY UPDATE http://www.calvarychapelkaneohe.com/index.php/teach/prophecy-updates/serie/10000

8/29/15

I had just finished my book and proudly announced it to my mom. I forwarded her the Daily Sapphires from Johnathan Cahn on X-Power, dated 082615. I checked this evening's E-mails and noticed this E-mail from Gaspar Anastasi at Word of Life Ministries (WOLM.NET). Isn't God marvelous?

"When It's Hard to Forgive

Recently I asked someone why they wouldn't forgive a particular person. The person had repented and asked for forgiveness, but they refused.

"Why did you refuse them?" I asked. "Because I could tell they weren't sincere. They really aren't sorry, so they don't deserve to be forgiven."

Is that what Jesus says? Hardly. "If you do not forgive men their sins, your Father will not forgive your sins." (Matt. 6:15)

Only those who truly recognize their own sin, and the price Jesus paid for them to be forgiven, can forgive those who sinned against them. At least we hope so. Forgiveness is hard, but so is reaping the results of not forgiving.

Every one of us who has experienced God's forgiveness is called to extend His love and forgiveness to others. He gives us grace, to show grace to others. He pours His love in us, to love like He does.

Often people say they've forgiven when the really haven't. They'll say over and over, "Yes, I've forgiven them," and then they tack on, "I just don't want to have anything to do with them." If they were really honest, they would admit that secretly they'd like to see that person pay a price for what they did.

Thankfully, that's not how God forgives us. When He forgives us, He wipes the slate clean and treats us like we never did what we really did. He doesn't keep a record of it to bring up at some future time. Jesus just doesn't forgive, He restores back what was lost.

When we forgive others as Jesus commands us to, we receive healing. He takes away the pain of the offense. To have the forgiveness worked in and through us we must do the following:

1. Pray for God to Bless the one who hurt us, however He sees fit.

2. Willingly choose to be a channel of God's love flowing from us to them.

3. Desire to see that person healed, restored

and serving again in the call God

has on their life.

In John 21:15-17, Jesus gives us His example of forgiving Peter. In the courtyard after Jesus' arrest, Peter had to face the fact that he denied Christ, not once, but 3 times. Now Jesus comes to Peter and confronts him.

"Simon son of John, do you love Me more than these?"

"Yes, Lord," he said, "you know that I love you."

Jesus said, "Feed my lambs."

Again Jesus said, "Simon son of John, do you love Me?"

He answered, "Yes, Lord, you know that I love you."

Jesus said, "Take care of my sheep."

The third time He aid to him, "Simon son of John, do you love Me?"

Peter was hurt because Jesus asked him a third time, "Do you love Me?"

He said, "Lord, you know all things; you know that I love you.

Jesus said, "Feed my sheep."

Interesting isn't it, that Peter denied Jesus 3 times, and Jesus gave Peter 3 chances to reaffirm his love for Him. Jesus was making a point here. No matter how many times we've fallen and denied Him, He's there to pick us up, forgive us and restore us.

Our receiving His forgiveness, nor our service to Him depends on us, but rather it has everything to do with what He's done for us. He's a God of restoration!

Our instruction from Jesus is the same He gave Peter, "Follow Me". As followers of Christ, we're to keep following Him and modeling His behavior.....especially in forgiving others. Yes, even though forgiveness is hard and comes with a cost.

Share your Heart: What would it cost you to follow Jesus' example and forgive someone who is so hard to forgive?

Your comments and testimonies are important to us.

Visit our blog page, www.GasparandMichele.com"